Vision from the Valleys

100 Daily devotions birthed out of the Welsh Revival and Apostolic Movement

Compiled by John Caldwell
Foreword by Alistair Matheson

Welsh valley sunset.
Image taken by Sian Belle Galbraith.
Used with permission.

Dedication

To Mrs. Cameron, and in memory of her late husband, Simon Cameron. May your legacy bear fruit, not only in this generation, but in the generations to come.

Acknowledgements

Thank you to Wendy Tomin, the daughter of Mrs. Cameron – without your offer of the books, this book would not exist! Thank you to Mrs. Cameron for kindly letting your husband's books go to a new home. Thank you to Alistair Matheson, for writing such an encouraging foreword. Thanks to my wife Laura for helping with the formatting – you zoomed through a task that would have taken me days! And finally thanks to those of you who agreed to read a draft and provide a word of endorsement – your input and encouragement is greatly appreciated. Above all, I want to thank God for his providence in bringing these old writings across my path, and stirring within me a desire to compile this book. To God be the Glory!

Commendations

A rich treasure of wisdom, inspiration and challenge that has been birthed in the crucible of revival and firmly rooted in scripture. A valuable addition to any devotional journey.

John Glass, former General Superintendent, Elim

John Caldwell's 'Vision from the Valleys' is a welcome addition to our understanding of what God did when he stirred the Welsh Revival into being in the first years of the twentieth century.

Men and women, many with limited formal education, carried to their nation and the world a revelation of Christ and his Church which was fresh and deep in equal measure.

Of course, each generation must discover the breath of God on truth, else the fresh becomes stale and the deep becomes shallow.

'Vision from the Valleys' takes us not to a moment in history, but allows us to glimpse into things eternal; 'Vision' takes us not to the Wales of a another era but to a setting into which for a season, at least, God's will was done on earth as in heaven.

May all who read be transported not back to a time and place now buried in history but propelled into a contemporary understanding and expression of God's love for the Church and his mission to reach all mankind with the Gospel.

This is the heritage of the Apostolic Church, its mantle to help carry and its mission to help fulfil.

Tim Jack, National Leader, Apostolic Church UK

As one who has found enormous inspiration from myriad stories of the Welsh Revival of 1904-5 (one of the most famed revivals in world history); as one who has studied a little the lives of Apostolic pioneers like Andrew Turnbull ('the Alexander Boddy of Scotland') for the chapter on Pentecostal Revivals in Scotland in the book, 'Glory in the Glen'; and as one who has had fond connections with an Apostolic congregation in the north-east of Scotland – the title and subtitle of this book immediately drew my attention. These devotional writings – from a plethora of mainly long-forgotten names – are deeply stirring and motivational. They express a fire and passion that appear to stem directly from those exciting days of the early 20th century.

Tom Lennie

Author of the trilogy of historical studies on Scottish Christian revivals: - *'Glory in the Glen'*, *'Land of Many Revivals'* and *'Scotland Ablaze'*.

I am so thankful to God that my formative years as a believer were spent in the Apostolic Church. I believe God has a great purpose for this amazing movement in these days. John Caldwell has certainly mined a rich vein of gold from these early pioneers. This wonderful book is a reminder of the deep spirituality these men walked in and is very much welcome in these days of shallowness and superficiality.

Bill McMurdo, Pastor, Glasgow Revival Centre

What a great resource. I was left with a sense of being a time traveller! The eternity of The Word of God. The insight of men and women, some close to 100 years ago. And, the immediacy of how much I felt that these were words for right now, Rhema. *Hebrews 4:12 (NLT) For the word of God is alive and powerful. It is sharper than the sharpest two-edged sword, cutting between soul and spirit, between joint and marrow. It exposes our innermost thoughts and desires.* I honestly feel this book demonstrates the truths in that amazing verse of Scripture.

It is eminently helpful, no matter how long you have been on your journey with Christ, if you use it for a daily devotion you will be enriched and challenged and I believe deeply touched. I loved that it was able to do this to me and yet it could take just a few minutes or I could spend longer, lingering on the "anything you feel God might be saying to you personally".

I have a sense that this is what would delight the original writers. That their thoughts and insights would encourage us today to engage with God for ourselves. Every "day" made me think, and surely that is the best recommendation anyone can give a Daily Devotional.

Thank you John Caldwell for drawing this together and making it available. My only problem is what do I do after 100 days? I'll be done by the turn of the year! Perhaps there will be a volume 2!

Eric Scott, Pastor, Perth Elim

Imagine what God can do through lives totally abandoned and surrendered to his purposes. Learn from past revivals in this great 100 day devotional and believe for even greater days ahead.

Andrew Smith - Gateway Church, Glasgow.

What an amazing Devotional! 'Vision from the Valleys' brings history back to life. When I read this, I was both disturbed and stirred. I felt myself transported back to my bible school days where I studied the Welsh revival. This brought back so many memories. As I heard about all the things that happened over a hundred years ago, as a young student, I was stirred and challenged; as I read this devotional I was stirred and challenged afresh!

Oh man, it's very dangerous to read this! It's dangerous because it's designed to get you out from where you are into new dimensions and a new walk with God. It challenges you to *be more*, to *do more* and *go further*! As a warning, if you want to stay where you are, don't buy this devotional, and don't read this book at all!

Sava Tomin, Founding Pastor, Kairos Church, Timisoara, Romania

Use this great devotional to stir your heart from the early days of the Apostolic Church. It really could be 100 days to fuel the fire in your heart!

Steve Uppal, All Nations Movement

Foreword

Serving as lead pastor of Glasgow City Church, my thoughts frequently turn to the testimony of its pioneering apostle, Andrew Turnbull. It was on the prompting of a prophetic word by his young lad, Thomas, that this man of God stepped out in faith, brought his family from the Scottish east coast to Armadale Street in Glasgow's Dennistoun in 1915, and founded what was originally called The Burning Bush in their living room.

Even the mention of our church's first name reminds me of God's pristine intention for His church: a place of divine encounter. Just as Moses was moved, or rather stopped, to utter the words, "I will turn aside now, and see this great sight ..."; and just as crowds arrested by tongues of fire on the Day of Pentecost were stirred to ask, "What does this mean? ..."; so throughout the history of His church – and even my small part of it – the ascended Christ has gifted light-bearers like the Turnbulls, the Williamses, the Lewises and many more, to compel our gaze and awaken us to the real, life-transforming substance of the spiritual truth they speak.

Giants of men upon whose shoulders I should aspire to stand. But today I'm happy to sit at their feet! And for such an opportunity, I am indebted to my friend, 21st century torch-bearer and voracious reader, John Caldwell, who, like a modern-day Ezra, just happened to bump into a near-ancient treasure trove of out-of-print Pentecostal publications, from which this selection has been so inspirationally compiled. Thank you, John! Now we can all sit at their feet. Who knows, some may even scale their shoulders.

Alistair J Matheson August, 2019

Introduction

Towards the end of the summer holidays of 2019, my wife and I packed our boys and dog into our car, to make our way to Peterhead, to visit Mrs. Cameron, the widow of the late Simon Cameron. We had been invited to come and take books from the late pastor's library.

That day was a special day. We received a lot more than books. We spent a few hours with Mrs. Cameron as she shared testimony after testimony concerning their experience of the power and presence of God.

Simon had been a Pentecostal pastor, and I had a gut feeling that there may have been some old Pentecostal gems within his library. I wasn't disappointed. My only regret was not having enough space to take more of his books. His library could have been used as resource for any theological college in the country – Simon read widely and richly. However – it was the Pentecostal classics that I was interested in. And I found some. Amongst the books were several very old editions of 'Riches of Grace' the printed books and booklets from the Apostolic Church UK – the earliest edition dating back to 1926.

The 'Apostolics' have a fascinating history. Apart from being the oldest Pentecostal denomination in the UK, historically they were different from the others (AoG and Elim) because of their emphasis on Apostles and Prophets. Ironically, the passing of time has been kind to the Apostolics due to the fresh emphasis on apostles and prophets, in recent decades, amongst the contemporary charismatic and pentecostal movements. The 'five-fold ministry' is now more widely accepted by pentecostals and charismatics of various stripes.

Anyway, as I flicked through these old writings that were hidden in-between old dusty book covers, and barely legible tiny font – I just felt I had to do something with these old writings.

These writings were just as anointed, prophetic, and relevant as they were at the time when they were written. And I felt they needed to be made accessible for a new generation.

As a bit of a history geek, I've resisted the urge to publish a historical academic work – although I may do that in the future. I felt this needed a wider audience. So, a devotional it is. Small bite-size chunks, carefully selected, and edited for the modern reader. At times I have reworded sections, all the while being careful to retain the original writer's thoughts but recognising the need to remove archaic terms that no longer make sense. I hope I have done this task justice. I've resisted the temptation to add my own commentary into the daily devotions. A couple of publishers advised me to do this in order to give each 'Day' more content. Whilst I value their input, I've decided not to do that. Personally, I feel that would detract from the purpose of the devotional. This devotional isn't about my reflections or meditations, it is about encountering what God has said through anointed vessels from the past.

All that remains to be said is – *I hope you enjoy the book.* I've provided a bit of a structure, but use it in the way that works for you. If you don't like using written prayers – ditch that part and just pray in your own words. If you have another Bible Reading Plan, don't worry about the Further Reading section. If, like me, you are a church history geek – feel free to mine the book for quotes from key leaders of the Apostolic Church UK. Or, if you do want to follow the book as it is designed – I pray that you will enjoy 100 days of blessing. I pray that something of the anointing from the words on the pages will settle upon you. I pray that you will have your own Burning Bush moment. Heaven knows the nations need a people of God who are ablaze with his glory.

John Caldwell
2019

The Welsh Revival and Apostolic Movement

The years 1904-5 saw a powerful revival sweep over Wales. The revival has been referred to, by many, as the greatest revival ever. Rick Joyner says: "A few spiritual awakenings in history have spanned the globe and touched millions, but it can be argued that none had as much concentrated power and impact as the Welsh Revival." Another description of the revival makes the following observations.

The story of the Welsh Revival is astounding. Begun with prayer meetings of less than a score of intercessors, when it burst its bounds the churches of Wales were crowded for more than two years. A hundred thousand outsiders were converted and added to the churches, the vast majority remaining true to the end. Drunkenness was immediately cut in half, and many taverns went bankrupt. Crime was so diminished that judges were presented with white gloves signifying that there were no cases of murder, assault, rape or robbery or the like to consider. The police became 'unemployed' in many districts. Stoppages occurred in coal-mines, not due to unpleasantness between management and workers, but because so many foul-mouthed miners became converted and stopped using foul language that the horses which hauled the coal trucks in the mines could no longer understand what was being said to them, and transportation ground to a halt.[1]

The revival meetings themselves were marked by a deep and intense presence of God.

The fact is, unless heard, it is unimaginable and when heard indescribable. There was no hymnbook. No one gave out a hymn. Just anyone would start the singing, and very rarely did it happen that the hymn started was out of harmony with the mood at the moment. Once started, as if moved by a simultaneous impulse, the hymn was caught up by the whole congregation almost as if what was about to be sung had been announced and all were responding to the baton of a visible human leader.

---

[1] Historian Edwin Orr

I have seen nothing like it. You felt that the thousand or fifteen hundred persons before you had become merged into one myriad-headed, but simple-souled personality. Such was the perfect blending of the mood and purpose that it bore eloquent testimony to a unity created only by the Spirit of God." Another witness testified: "The praying and singing were both wonderful. There was no need for an organ. The assembly was its own organ as a thousand sorrowing or rejoicing hearts found expression in the Psalmody of their native hills.[2]

The vessel that God laid his hand upon in the revival was a young miner called Evan Roberts. Roberts, having gone through a deep dealing with God, where he cried out, "Bend me! Bend me! Bend me!" is said to have prophesied the revival:

I have had a vision of all Wales being lifted up to heaven. We are going to see the mightiest revival that Wales has ever known - the Holy Spirit is coming just now. We must be ready. We must have a little band and go all over the country preaching.[3]

James Alexander Stewart referred to the revival as "The invasion of Wales by the Spirit through Evan Roberts." Another source says, "The presence of God was felt everywhere. The atmosphere was divinely charged. People seemed to be convicted of sin and become aware of the need of salvation, even without the presence of a preacher or evangelist."

---

[2] R.B. Jones

[3] Evan Roberts.

The Apostolic Church

Stories of the Welsh Revival abound and are known by many. What is perhaps less known to many is the fact that the Welsh Revival gave birth to the Apostolic Church. A movement which would start in Pennygroes, spread to the Welsh Valleys, and throughout Wales, from there it would gather momentum throughout the British Isles, eventually spreading its rivers throughout the globe.

From small beginnings in 1913, when God set apart the man who would be the primary leader in the movement – Daniel Powell Williams (D.P. Williams), to 1959, the movement had literally spread all over the world and there were Apostolic Churches in Australia, Canada, Denmark, France, Germany, Ghana, India, Italy, New Zealand, Nigeria, Norway, Switzerland, USA, Jamaica and many more parts of the world.

The Apostolic Church was birthed in the Welsh revival and a number of its early leaders and members were men and women who had been saved during the Welsh revival. Following the Welsh revival there was a season of 'new' and unusual manifestations of the Holy Spirit. Speaking in tongues, healings, and prophesying began to occur in various places throughout the world where people were seeking a move of the Spirit. Many who were converted during the Welsh revival were later 'baptised in the Holy Spirit' during this next wave of the Spirit in 1907-8.[4] This was the start of the world-wide Pentecostal movement.

However, with the Apostolic Church, the Lord was doing something even more unique. Whilst many Pentecostals were happy to embrace speaking in tongues, prophesying, healing and deliverance, the Apostolics believed in a full restoration of New Testament gifts including Apostles and Prophets. Most Pentecostals were wary of this and maintained existing presbyterian or congregational forms of government, but the Apostolics sought to restore the five-fold ministry as taught by Paul the Apostle in Ephesians 4. Ironically, over a hundred years later, most of the Pentecostal groups who were once suspicious of Apostles and Prophets have now come to embrace the five-fold ministry. In many ways the Apostolics were a pioneering people who were ahead of their time.

---

[4] *What God hath wrought,* T.N Turnbull, p13.

Some of the names you will encounter in this devotional were prominent leaders in the Apostolic Church, and their stories have been retained. If you want to find out more about them you can read T.N. Turnbull's 'What God hath Wrought' or Gordon Weeks' 'Chapter Thirty Two: Part of a History of the Apostolic Church 1900-2000'. Others have long been forgotten other than their writings which are retained in whatever copies remain of 'Riches of Grace'. In some ways, this devotional reflects the 'nameless and faceless' aspect of the apostolic revival – which should be the characteristic of any true apostolic work. Ephesians 4 tells us that the five-fold ministry exists to equip the saints for works of service. True apostolic Christianity is not the Christianity of the celebrity pastor, prophet, apostle or evangelist – true apostolic Christianity serves, equips, and releases the body of Christ to do the ministry of Christ. With that being said, the Lord blessed the Apostolic Church with some powerful leaders, a number of whom appear in this devotional. Before we turn to their teaching, let us get a glimpse of their lives.

The Leaders

The founder of the movement was, as mentioned earlier, a young Daniel Powell Williams, a miner who was converted during the revival in 1904. D.P Williams would go on to become an apostle, and the first President of the Church Council. He was called to ministry through God speaking prophetically; it is no coincidence that the prophetic ministry would mark his life and the life of the Apostolic Church. The Lord spoke to Williams directly, "Are you willing to go and preach the unsearchable riches of Christ, to forsake all, and follow me?" It was a crisis moment for Williams. He had hoped to become an ordained minister, but it seemed the Lord had a less conventional route in store for the young man.

In 1910, two men from London were told by the Lord to go and anoint "the Lord's servant" at a farm, where a number of people would be gathered. No human plans had been put in place for this. It was orchestrated by the Holy Spirit. Afterwards the Lord used D.P. Williams to prophesy over his brother, W.J. Williams, the consequence was that W.J. Williams was also brought into the ministry of the apostolic church where the two brothers served the Lord faithfully as apostle and prophet. Despite being a powerful leader who pioneered a movement, D.P Williams was a man who was known for his gentleness and ability to unite the church – even in the midst of difficult seasons. D.P. and W.J. Williams were both key players in spreading the movement to the nations.

Whilst God was dealing with the Joneses in Wales, he was also dealing with Andrew Turnbull in Glasgow, H.V. Chanter in Bradford, and Pastor F. Hodges in Hereford. All of these men were in the process of arriving at apostolic convictions and would join the Apostolic movement and each one would play a key part. In Bradford, along with Chanter, God was also raising up other leaders with apostolic convictions, among them: A Rhodes, G. Perfect, and H. Cousen.

Andrew Turnbull has been described by revival historian, Tom Lennie, as "Scotland's Alexander Boddy". The following account will give a glimpse into the depth and power of Turnbull's ministry.

Scotland, the land of the Covenanters, is another country where it has pleased God to pioneer many Apostolic Churches...The first leaders of the work, Andrew Turnbull, J. Larkins, J. MacPherson, and T.N. Turnbull made plans to extend the church in obedience to prophecy, and opened churches in the towns and villages of Scotland. What our eyes saw in those days in the saving of precious souls, the healing of bodies, the casting out of demons, the outpouring of the Holy Spirit, will never be forgotten. In a 12-month period 100 people were baptised in the Glasgow Assembly.[5]

Andrew Turnbull's ministry seems to have been marked by powerful miracles. Many testimonies of healing can be sourced back to the ministry of Andrew Turnbull. Florence M. Leadbetter gave the following testimony in 1931. Here she reports being healed of a dislocated spine.

As a young girl I met with a serious accident which partially dislocated my spine, and set up inflammation. For months I was bed-ridden, and although able to crawl about afterwards, for thirteen years at intervals, I suffered intense pain. I was examined by several doctors, who said they could do nothing for me – that all I could do was rest. About ten years ago, I was having an especially bad time with my spine. Again I consulted a doctor, but he too admitted he could do nothing to help me. About this time, pastors A. Turnbull and Larkins were conducting meetings in Stromness, where I was then residing. I had not thought of Divine healing until I heard it preached, then I knew that Jesus could heal me. Pastor Turnbull came and laid his hands on my head, a fire shot through all my body, and all pain vanished. Before he had even prayed, my healing had been accomplished. This happened nearly ten years ago, and I have never had any pain in my spine since. Jesus healed me, and Jesus alone! Praise his name![6]

Signs and wonders were a part of the Apostolic Church revival. The account of Frank Hodges' Baptism in the Spirit, with signs following, is a case in point.

---

[5] Ibid. p40.

[6] Riches of Grace, Vol. V11, P33.

Pastor F. Hodges, Hereford, received a powerful baptism in the Spirit, in the latter days of the outpouring. He was on a mountain in Wales, with another brother, and they were seeking God. Accompanying his baptism was the ability to speak in the Welsh language – this was confirmed by witnesses who heard him.[7]

Similarly, on three occasions, Pastor John Cardwell spoke in Welsh whilst speaking in tongues. Similar experiences were said to have happened in Nigeria amongst various tribes – it was reported that leaders would bring a word in tongues and it would be understood by different tribes who heard the message.[8]

In addition to testimonies about tongues there are testimonies about fulfilled prophecies – including one about the outcome of the War which was given in 1940. Prophecies were also accurately given about the establishment of Apostolic Churches oversees.

Not only were there fulfilled prophecies, there were many testimonies of healing and deliverance. N.T Turnbull gives many examples in his book, *What God hath wrought,* of the sick being healed, demons being cast out and people experiencing the presence of God. Turnbull gives the following account of a miracle that made an impression upon him.

> Perhaps the most outstanding miracle I have ever seen was that of a cripple in Glasgow. George Braindard was a pensioner from the army, and one of his legs had no life in it. He could stick needles into it without pain. One of the members of the Glasgow church, asked him to come to the assembly, which invitation he accepted. He had to be carried up the two stairs to the church hall, and at the end of the service gave his heart to Christ. Afterwards he asked for prayer for healing, and when this was done, and hands were laid upon him, his knee bent for the first time for many months. Then in the name of Jesus Christ, he was commanded to walk, and soon he was not only walking but running up and down the aisle of the church.[9]

---

[7] Ibid. p150.

[8] Ibid. p151.

[9] Ibid. 146.

Many more stories could be told. If you want to read more, I encourage you to get the books by Turnbull and Weeks. Having seen something of the context and background which gave birth to the Apostolic movement, let us now turn to the teachings, prophetic words, and interpretations of tongues which were born in the fires of revival. Keeping in mind, we don't visit these works in the way that tourists visit a museum – with romantic imaginations about the past; we come instead to a living fountain to drink deeply of truths that were given through the eternal Spirit of God. We also come prayerfully with a longing in our hearts for God to do it again in our day. Come Holy Spirit!

Once more Lord, once more Lord;
As in the days of yore;
On these dear lands, Thy Spirit pour,
Set the nations now on fire.[10]

---

[10] Adaption of a Scottish Hymn.

Day 1: The Valley

Further reading
Psalm 23

Lord, even when your path takes me through the valley of deepest darkness, fear will never conquer me, for you already have! You remain close to me and lead me through it all the way. Your authority is my strength and my peace. The comfort of your love takes away my fear. I'll never be lonely, for you are near. Psalm 23:4 (TPT)

When many of you are in the Valley, you will receive an experience that is given to the individual, that not only benefits you, but others who come into contact with you will benefit also. For it is written, "When you go through the Valley, I will be with you." And there are experiences in the Valley that are given to the individual that are given to carry him or her into the blessings that are beyond. Everyone went through the Valley; and so you must also go through the Valley. [11]

(Thomas Turnbull)

Jot down anything you feel God might be saying to you personally.

_____

_____

_____

_____

_____

_____

Lord, thank you for the valleys I face in life. The valleys are not a sign of your absence; they are a sign of your presence. In the valley you are with me, you draw me close to you, you strip away all that hinders, and you are equipping me to be a source of blessing for others. Amen.

---

[11] (The Word of the Lord through the Prophet Thomas Turnbull, Scotland, 1st Aug 1926).

Day 2: Do not Panic

Further reading
Exodus 14

Moses answered the people, "Do not be afraid. Stand firm and you will see the deliverance the Lord will bring you today. The Egyptians you see today you will never see again. The Lord will fight for you; you need only to be still." Exodus 14:13-14 (NIV)

When you are having obstacles and difficulties in both the local and wider church, or in your experience, do not be afraid of Pharaoh and his hosts. If you are with God, leave it between God and the devil; God will manage him alright. But we are stirred up, and disturbed; we lose patience; and faith; and we are tested to the uttermost, and we think it's all over, when the very next step is the step that God takes to make a display of his character in a glorious manner, to put the devil to shame.[12]

(D.P. Williams)

Jot down anything you feel God might be saying to you personally.

_____

_____

_____

_____

_____

_____

Father, forgive me when I allow trouble and trials to cause me to take my eyes off you. You are faithful, and all-powerful. You have every situation I face, in-hand, and under control. Help me rest in you. Amen.

---

[12] D.P Williams. Exposition, 2nd August 1926).

Day 3: Word and Spirit

Further reading
Luke 24

And they said one to another, Did not our heart burn within us, while he talked with us by the way, and while he opened to us the scriptures? Luke 24:32 (KJV)

We realise that there are depths in inspiration that we must be inspired to fathom, and to dive in to. There are many that read the blessed Book day after day; they use it on the surface, superficially, and as they are not in tenor with the inspiration of the Book they see nothing in the Word of God. But when we are in fellowship with God, through the Holy Spirit who has produced the Book, then the Book becomes divine substance and nourishment to our souls; power and fire and light and energy and victory in our lives.[13]

(D.P Williams)

Jot down anything you feel God might be saying to you personally.

_____

_____

_____

_____

_____

_____

Lord, let me not simply approach your word in an intellectual manner. Help me to encounter your presence as I read the scriptures. Let me not only hear your voice, let me feel your breath as I meditate upon your Word.

---

[13] D.P Williams. Exposition, 3rd August 1926).

Day 4: God is Sovereign

Further reading
1 Timothy 4

That is why we labour and strive, because we have put our hope in the living God, who is the Saviour of all people, and especially of those who believe." 1 Tim 4:10 (NIV)

God is sovereign! "Demas has left me"; "All have turned away in Asia" – Paul had laboured very hard there: "never-the-less" the aged apostle declares, "lay it not to their charge." God was with him. When seemingly everything was coming to the ground and the Visitation of God the Holy Spirit in previous years coming to seeming disaster, God's sovereign will was over-ruling everything, every circumstance, controlling every current, because he had foreseen everything from Eternity. May God enable us to make our Divine Election sure; enlighten us in His Divine Purpose, so that we may rule with him here and now, believing steadfastly, that He is sovereign over all, over-ruling all things for His own glory. Amen![14]

(W.H. Lewis)

Jot down anything you feel God might be saying to you personally.

_____

_____

_____

_____

_____

_____

Lord, when it all seems to "go to the ground" help me remember that you are sovereign, and you are with me – and you are bringing good out every situation. When everything seems to be going wrong, help me remember that nothing can undermine your purpose.

---

[14] Apostle, W.H. Lewis, London 3rd August 1926.

Day 5: God is never late!

Further reading
Genesis 18

Is anything too difficult for the Lord? At the appointed time I will return to you... Gen 18:14 (NASB)

Our God is never behind time. When we are quaking with fear, that is the time when God exhibits his strength. When troubles become seven times more than they have been, He gives seven times more strength. Our God is equal to the need every time.[15]
(Andrew Turnbull)

Look at the power which works in my own people. Look! I the Lord have come into your heart. Anything that is from your natural strength will fail. But if I am working in you, everything that comes to pass shall be of me – as it has been said, "If it be of God it shall not fail." Because I am with you, and my power is at your disposal, there is no need for you quake at this time.[16]

(Thomas Turnbull)

Jot down anything you feel God might be saying to you personally.

_____

_____

_____

_____

_____

_____

Thank you Lord, your timing is perfect. Help me to see that when trouble comes, this is simply an opportunity for me to see your power at work.

---

[15] Apostle Andrew Turnbull, Scotland, 8th August 1926.

[16] Prophet Thomas Turnbull, Scotland, 8th August, 1926.

Day 6: Alleluia of Electing Grace

Further reading
Revelation 19

Then I heard *something* like the voice of a great multitude and like the sound of many waters and like the sound of mighty peals of thunder, saying, "Hallelujah! For the Lord our God, the Almighty, reigns. Revelation 19:6 (NASB)

This is the Alleluia of Electing Grace. God Omnipotent has a Bridegroom ready: He is Jesus, whom we know and love, and who came by His Spirit in Wales in the revival of 1904, and saved so many from the gutter (and so many from the pulpits, and from the "Set fawr"; and from among the Pharisees and scribes, as well as from the ditches): that blessed Jesus who is now walking here and throughout our land. May God give us all a revelation of his wonderful purpose; for he is calling out a people by the Spirit, a Bride for himself, a Body of People, a company of Saints.[17]

(W.T. Evans)

Jot down anything you feel God might be saying to you personally.

_____

_____

_____

_____

_____

_____

Come Lord Jesus! Come once again in revival power, not only in Wales, but throughout the UK and the wider world. Pour out your Spirit afresh; bring in the harvest. Amen.

---

[17] W.T. Evans, Evangelist, Pontypridd, 8th August, 1926.

Day 7: Be filled with the Holy Spirit

Further reading
Ephesians 5

And be not drunk with wine, wherein is excess; but be filled with the Spirit Ephesians 5:18 (KJV)

The Perfumer of Heaven is the Holy Spirit. God wishes to beautify his people for the King's palace. We are going to spend a long time with Him…God wishes to live his character in you and me. All outward manifestations are valueless without this life of God within. People are clamouring (as of old) for miracles, and to see the dead raised; but what God wants is to build in you and me his divine character…The beautifying process of the Holy Spirit works from within the spirit outwardly.[18]

(Wm. Taylor)

Jot down anything you feel God might be saying to you personally.

_____

_____

_____

_____

_____

_____

Come Holy Spirit! Fill my life afresh. Fill me to overflowing so that the character of Christ may be formed deep within that he may shine through me. Anoint me afresh as I surrender to you. Change my desires – may I long for you and you alone. The Christian life is impossible without you. Holy Spirit, lead me into the fullness of the life of Christ. Amen.

---

[18] Pastor Wm. Taylor, (Porth) 3rd August 1927.

Day 8: Spiritual Realities

Further reading
Exodus 31

The anointing oil also, and the fragrant incense for the holy place, they are to make them according to all that I have commanded you." Exodus 31:11 (NASB)

When we are attacked by the enemy (as the man on the road to Jericho) the Holy Spirit as oil or ointment soothes the bruises, and we are strengthened in spirit, and our praise ascends. God lives in the praises of His saints. When the saints sing, they are not alone, for the invisible choirs of heaven sing with them. In the church, the five-gifted ministry of Jesus is in operation, and the character of the Head is being moulded in his Body. Let God the Holy Spirit, do his work in anointing, beautifying, and soothing, so that Jesus may see the travail of his soul, and so that he might find faith on the earth when He returns.[19]

(Pastor Wm. Taylor)

Jot down anything you feel God might be saying to you personally.

_____

_____

_____

_____

_____

_____

Lord, your presence changes everything. When afflicted by the enemy – your Spirit soothes and heals my soul. Let my song rise today like incense – no matter what I face. Amen.

---

[19] Pastor Wm. Taylor, (Porth) 3rd August 1927

Day 9: The Spirit's Influence

Further reading
Acts 2

They were all filled and equipped with the Holy Spirit. Acts 2:4 (TPT)

Be filled with the Spirit. Ephesians 5:18 (KJV)

It is God's delight to fill His people with the Holy Spirit. Paul tells the people of God to "Be filled with the Spirit." The text is addressed to believing Christians, who although baptised with the Holy Spirit, are exhorted to "Be filled with the Spirit." The danger is that we look back upon our baptism, and have a tendency to treat it as a goal, rather than a gate. Even as a drunken person is under the influence of another power, so we must be filled with the Spirit, completely under His influence and out of ourselves.[20]

(J.F.D. Thompson)

Jot down anything you feel God might be saying to you personally.

_____

_____

_____

_____

_____

_____

Lord, forgive me for viewing the baptism of the Holy Spirit as a goal, rather than a gateway. Let me not stand at this gate marvelling at yesterday's experience, let me push through the gate into your fullness for today.

---

[20] J.F.D. Thompson, Elder, 3rd August 1927.

Day 10: A Prophecy about Hell

Further reading
Matthew 10

And fear not them which kill the body, but are not able to kill the soul: but rather fear him which is able to destroy both soul and body in hell. Matthew 10:28 (KJV)

The great purpose of the enemy at the present is to minimise eternal punishment, and his great purpose in this is because he knows it will cause more apathy, so far as the sinner is concerned, and cause my servants to preach less of the truth of Christ. If my servants realised for one minute in their heart of hearts, and if my people as a whole realised, the terribleness of the wrath of God, the fiery indignation God must send against sin and the things of sin, if they realised the position the sinner was in and the awful *looking-forward-to* of judgement, your heart would be torn in two crying for men and women to be saved. Your preaching would be more effective, and your desire to come to the meetings, to go to the open-air, and to go out and tell the people on the street would be more intense.[21]

(Prophetic Ministry, Glasgow)

Jot down anything you feel God might be saying to you personally.

_____

_____

_____

_____

_____

_____

Lord, let me not lose sight of your holiness, justice and wrath. May they move me to deeper holiness and love for the lost.
Amen.

---

[21] Prophetic ministry, Glasgow, 1931, Prophetical Ministry, p23-26.)

Day 11: The Closer Walk

Further reading
James 4

Move your heart closer and closer to God, and he will come even closer to you. James 4:8 (TPT)

Oh my people! Press in closer to hear my words. Come closer to see what I am doing. There are many that are on the outside of the camp that are crying for me to give them a greater vision. But my answer is this – it is not the "greater vision" they need, but a CLOSER WALK. There are many that want to have better sight to see; but the distance is TOO FAR between them and me, and I am not likely to give them greater sight when they are able to come closer. And if you will hear and see, then you must come closer, and press towards ME: THE CENTRE.[22]

(W.A. Rowe)

Jot down anything you feel God might be saying to you personally.

_____

_____

_____

_____

_____

_____

Lord, I recognise that longing for greater vision, or faith, or discernment is not the same as longing for you. Forgive me if I have put 'spiritual' things before you. Oh Lord. I recognise that I can make an idol out of spiritual things. Help me seek you first, and everything else will flow out of my intimacy with you.
Amen.

---

[22] Prophet, W.A. Rowe, Hereford, 3rd August 1927.

Day 12: The Principle of the Cross

Further reading
John 12

Truly, truly, I say to you, unless a grain of wheat falls into the earth and dies, it remains alone; but if it dies, it bears much fruit. John 12:24 (ESV)

I would say to you, says the Lord, that with all my purposes there must be a seeming death before a life and fruitfulness. And there are times even when with my purposes I must bring you to know that they must die in your midst. You must be willing to see them "die" to "not die", says the Lord. For out of the "death" shall come the "abundant life." Oh my people! I promise you that if you see, what looks like my purposes coming to the dust, let it be known from the depth of Calvary, there shall be a rising to the heights of the throne, and from the seeming weakness of my dying, when you look back you see that same vision rising from the depths to new heights.[23]

(W.A. Rowe)

Jot down anything you feel God might be saying to you personally.

_____

_____

_____

_____

_____

_____

Thank you Lord for teaching me and showing me that death is not the end. In Jesus' death and resurrection we see your ways of working. Thank you, that even when my hopes and plans seem to have died, you are in fact using this death in order to raise up your purposes in my life.

---

[23] Prophet, W.A. Rowe, Hereford, 3rd August 1927.

Day 13: Resurrection Power

Further reading
Philippians 3

That I may know Him and the power of His resurrection, and the fellowship of His sufferings, being conformed to His death. Philippians 3:10 (NKJV)

When we are baptised with the Holy Spirit, we receive power, and that power has come first of all to deal with us. I have had to learn this: that with every call there is a death, no matter what we have been called in to, whether elders or deacons, we have to die in that calling before we can know God in it. When God has called certain people into certain ministries they have to go into a "death" experience. So it is with every calling in the church, every ministry must die in it, that we may be raised to newness of life that we may receive this resurrection experience in our lives.[24]

(H.V. Chanter)

Jot down anything you feel God might be saying to you personally.

_____

_____

_____

_____

_____

_____

I praise you Lord for the principles of the cross and the resurrection. Help me to embrace the cross and not to shrink from it. Help me to embrace the crucified life. Enable me to die with Christ, that I might live in the power of his resurrection. Thank you for the honour of sharing in Christ's sufferings and the sure hope that the sufferings of Christ lead to the life of Christ.
Amen.

---

[24] Apostle, H.V. Chanter, Bradford, 4th August 1927.

Day 14: The Power of Praise

Further reading
Psalm 149

Praise ye the Lord. Praise God in his sanctuary: praise him in the firmament of his power. Praise him for his mighty acts: praise him according to his excellent greatness...Praise him with the timbrel and dance: praise him with stringed instruments and organs. Praise him upon the loud cymbals: praise him upon the high sounding cymbals. Let everything that hath breath praise the Lord. Praise ye the Lord. Psalm 150 (KJV)

I rejoice to see a group of believers so taken up with the beauty of the Lord Jesus Christ that they can dance before him. I believe in it. It has a power of blessing. I believe that the power of praise and worship brings victory. If we want to live an overcoming life and a life of victory it must be by the way of praise. You will never get there by seeing the dark side every time. The power of praise is the power that will get you through the situation.[25]

(H.V. Chanter)

Jot down anything you feel God might be saying to you personally.

_____

_____

_____

_____

_____

_____

Lord, deliver me from formalism and tradition. Help me to see that true worship is less about formality, and more about extravagant praise and adoration of the God who is worthy to be praised! Amen.

---

[25] Apostle, H.V. Chanter, Bradford, 4th August 1927.

Day 15: Kept by God's Purpose

Further reading
Romans 8

And we know that in all things God works for the good of those who love him, who have been called according to his purpose. Romans 8:28 (NIV)

Joseph of old was kept by God even though he faced the pit and the prison. Why? Not because his dreams had been made known to him. Rather it was because God's purposes that were contained in those dreams were in the balance. Joseph was given faith to receive them; faith to communicate; and co-work with them, even though the path of his cooperation ran through the pit, and meant for him shame, prison and scorn. Nevertheless he was given an active faith which enabled him to move from his far-away home to a strange land. Why? Because GOD'S PURPOSE dwelt in him.[26]

(W. Jones Williams)

Jot down anything you feel God might be saying to you personally.

_____

_____

_____

_____

_____

_____

Sovereign God, you rule over all things, and you cause all things to work together for the good of your people and the glory of your name. Forgive me when I only see the problems and forget to see the providence. Forgive me when pain causes me to lose sight of your plan. You are good, and you are always working in every situation. Amen.

---

[26] Prophet W. Jones Williams, 4th August 1927.

35

Day 16: The Need for Christ

Further reading
Colossians 1

For in him all the fullness of God was pleased to dwell, and through him to reconcile to himself all things, whether on earth or in heaven, making peace by the blood of his cross. Colossians 1:19-20 (ESV)

The writer to the Colossians was full of Christ, he took all occasions to exalt the One he loved and adored. Oh that we also may be filled afresh with his Spirit, for he is coming soon for his church, and we read that when he does come he is going to receive his church to himself as a glorious church, without spot or wrinkle. In the light of this let us compare ourselves with Christ and by the Spirit and we shall soon see our individual need. It is only what he does through us that will remain; we are nothing apart from him.[27]

(V. Wellings)

Jot down anything you feel God might be saying to you personally.

_____

_____

_____

_____

_____

_____

Thank you Jesus that you are all in all, your grace is sufficient. You are all I need. You are my righteousness, wisdom, sanctification and redemption. Help me to live by your power and strength, and not my own. Amen.

---

[27] Pastor V. Wellings, 1958.

Day 17: Praying for Revival

Further reading
Psalm 85

'This is what I will do in the last days—I will pour out my Spirit on everybody and cause your sons and daughters to prophesy, and your young men will see visions, and your old men will experience dreams from God. Acts 2:17 (TPT)

I believe that God is working and preparing for a mighty revival. I believe God is arranging that those that will pray for it shall be in the midst of it. Oh for a mighty revival and for an outpouring of the Spirit amongst us…Oh for the Breath of God to pass over the borders of the nations, and spread over the whole world. And when we see it, after we have interceded for it, and the blessing is there, with tears streaming down our cheeks and with joy in our hearts we shall say, "For this I prayed!"[28]

(Percy G Parker)

Jot down anything you feel God might be saying to you personally.

_____

_____

_____

_____

_____

_____

Father in Heaven, plant within me a deep desire to pray for revival. More than that – send revival but start in me. Revive me with a touch from heaven that will spread to others. Help me to be a carrier of your presence wherever I go. May those who meet me, meet the Christ within me. Amen.

---

[28] Pastor, Percy G. Parker, 1939, Floods upon the dry ground, p64-65.

Day 18: Holy Surrender

Further reading
Exodus 3

Behold, the bush burned with fire, and the bush was not consumed. And Moses said, I will now turn aside, and see this great sight, why the bush is not burnt...God called unto him out of the midst of the bush, and said, Moses, Moses. And he said, Here am I. And he said, Draw not nigh hither: put off thy shoes from off thy feet, for the place whereon thou standest is holy ground. Exodus 3:2-5 (KJV)

I will reveal myself to you at this time. I have commenced to reveal myself and I will give you a fresh revelation of myself, and of my goodness, and of my purpose – but you must realise that it is the Lord, that this is Holy Ground, then you will take your shoes from off your feet, then when you take your shoes from off your feet, I am calling upon you that you will bow in humility, that you shall yield up, and surrender, that I may have my own way with you.[29]

(W.A.C Rowe)

Jot down anything you feel God might be saying to you personally.

_____

_____

_____

_____

_____

_____

Lord, help me to draw near to you in Spirit and in Truth. Here I am Lord – change me, fill me, send me. Amen.

---

[29] Pastor W.A.C. Rowe, 1939, Floods, p67.

Day 19: Humble yet Exalted

Further reading
Ruth 4

I have also acquired Ruth the Moabite, Mahlon's widow, as my wife, in order to maintain the name of the dead with his property, so that his name will not disappear from among his family or from his hometown. Today you are witnesses! Ruth 4:10 (NIV)

Ruth kept humble, but another one exalted her to a high position. Think of it! From a "Gleaner" to the wife of Boaz. What a calling. As Boaz' wife, she would be looked up to, and talked about, but flattery did not turn Ruth's head. When she felt proud, she looked back and remembered the experiences through which God had brought her. If we keep humble, God is sure to exalt us some time. We often wonder, is it worth going through? We have so much to withstand. Yes! Praise God it is worth it. Think about the things that God has prepared for us. At God's right hand, there are pleasures forever more.[30]

(Ruby Doidge)

Jot down anything you feel God might be saying to you personally.

_____

_____

_____

_____

_____

_____

Father, help me to be like Ruth when I face seasons of humbling. Today, I place my trust in you, knowing that you will provide every need. Amen.

---

[30] Ruby Doidge, Dumfries, Scotland, 1933. Riches of Grace September.

Day 20: The Living Church

Further reading
Revelation 1

And in the midst of the seven candlesticks one like unto the Son of man, clothed with a garment down to the foot, and girt about the paps with a golden girdle…and out of his mouth went a sharp two edged sword: and his countenance was as the sun shineth in his strength. Rev 1:13-16 (KJV)

What is the church to us? It is not merely a building, a mere form of service, nor is it a gathering together of saints, and Jesus in the midst. See the picture of the church in Revelation chapter 1. Jesus then, in the midst, *with his spoken word*, is our vision of the church. There are many people longing for it but they don't know about it. Tell them that which we enjoy in the presence of God. Tell them that Jesus is still here in the midst of his people, speaking to them.[31]

(H. Cousen)

Jot down anything you feel God might be saying to you personally.

_____

_____

_____

_____

_____

_____

All-glorious, ever-living and Almighty Jesus Christ you are the God who speaks. You are majestic in glory. I bow in adoration of you. I exalt you King Jesus – speak Lord, your servant is listening! Amen.

---

[31] General Superintendent, H. Cousen, Bradford, prophetic ministry, Floods p120-121.

Day 21: The Glory (Part 1)

Further reading
1 Peter 1

You love him passionately although you did not see him, but through believing in him you are saturated with an ecstatic joy, indescribably sublime and immersed in glory. 1 Peter 1:8 (TPT)

Looking up the meaning of the word "Glory" in the dictionary – I came across these: "Exultant with joy" and "weight of His presence". It is this aspect of Glory I wish to speak about. Many get a bit stale and the tendency is to lose the glory and lapse back into formality, even after receiving the baptism of the Spirit. The church in general has lost her glory, but the Lord is bringing it back to those individuals who will receive it, and through them he will ultimately permeate the church, making it a glorious church.[32]

(Frank Hodges)

Jot down anything you feel God might be saying to you personally.

_____

_____

_____

_____

_____

_____

Lord, let me be one of those whose hearts are burning with the glory of God. Forgive me for letting the fire die down. Fan into flame the glory of God in my spirit. Let your glory flood my soul. Let me be a channel for your glory to flow out and touch others. Jesus, restore your glory to the church, come with holy fire and consume us with your fiery love and holiness. Amen.

---

[32] Pastor Frank Hodges, 1939, Floods p134-136.

Day 22: The Glory (Part 2)

Further reading
2 Corinthians 3

For the Lord God is a sun and shield: the Lord will give grace and glory: no good thing will he withhold from them that walk uprightly. Psalm 84:11 (KJV)

The prayer of Paul in Eph 3:16 was "that he would grant you according to his riches of his glory to be strengthened with might by His Spirit in the inner man." So, it is with Glory that he strengthens us. Many Christians know about grace, and can talk about grace, but when you come to speak to them about glory, they know nothing about it in experience. It was never intended that the church should lose her glory, but like many things, her glory was lost through apostasy. Thank God for the truth which is to set you free: The Glory strengthens you, and the Glory changes you. "But we all, with open face beholding as in a glass the glory of the Lord, are changed into the same image from glory to glory, even as by the Spirit of the Lord." (2 Cor. 3:18)[33]

(Frank Hodges)

Jot down anything you feel God might be saying to you personally.

_____

_____

_____

_____

_____

_____

Lord God, forgive me for separating your grace from your glory. Help me see that the experiential reality of your glory is at the heart of your purposes for your people. Amen.

---

[33] Pastor Frank Hodges, 1939, Floods p134-136.

Day 23: The Glory (Part 3)

Further reading
Isaiah 60

Arise, shine; for thy light is come, and the glory of the Lord is risen upon thee. Isaiah 60:1 (KJV)

The Lord wants to manifest his glory, in his people, and through his people. If you have received the baptism in the Spirit, it came from the Glory. It is the Ascension blessing of the glorified Lord. He imparts his glory in the baptism…There is no such thing as a silent Pentecost. Where the power of God is operative, there will be movement, power and glory. The baptism of the Spirit is a much bigger thing than we have thought it was. We are baptised into a power which is much bigger than ourselves. It is an immersion which is continuous into the trinity: for there is one God. In this baptism we come to know in a special way the love of the Father, the life of the Son, and the power of the Holy Spirit.[34]

(Frank Hodges)

Jot down anything you feel God might be saying to you personally.

_____

_____

_____

_____

_____

_____

Thank you, Jesus, for the gift of the Holy Spirit. Thank you for this impartation of Glory. Help me to be continually immersed in your Spirit – draw me deeper into the fellowship of the Trinity. Amen.

---

[34] Pastor Frank Hodges, 1939, Floods p134-136.

Day 24: Wind and Fire

Further reading
Acts 1

But you will receive power when the Holy Spirit has come upon you, and you will be my witnesses in Jerusalem and in all Judea and Samaria, and to the end of the earth." Acts 1:8 (ESV)

Do you turn to the later chapters of Acts? Do you love to see revival, when the evangelists declared the word and many were slain of the Lord, and there were manifestations of life and power? Do you love these chapters? Do you love to see the river of blessing? If you want to know how to keep it, you must walk up stream! You must walk upstream to the source. What is the source? Ah! Will you not find it in the early chapters? How can you expect the manifestations of the later chapters of Acts without going to the source of the early chapters? The blessing you find in Samaria is the blessing that was born earlier on. Ah! Revival is born in wind and fire. Wind and fire that will enter your heart and give you victory! Wind and fire! You cannot have the revival of the later chapters without the experience of Pentecost. It cannot be done. Revivals are born, not made.[35]

(W.A.C. Rowe)

Jot down anything you feel God might be saying to you personally.

_____

_____

_____

_____

_____

_____

Lord, let the wind blow, let the fire fall, let the Glory come down!

---

[35] Prophetical Ministry by Pastor W.A.C. Rowe, 1937.

Day 25: Shout to the Lord!

Further reading
Joshua 6

And it came to pass at the seventh time, when the priests blew with the trumpets, Joshua said unto the people, Shout; for the Lord hath given you the city. Joshua 6:16 (KJV)

Let your heart burn within you when I declare to you that I AM UNCHANGEABLY THE SAME. It is only my IMMUTIBILITY that will bring comfort. I would have my people of Zion shout and rejoice in my protection. GO FORWARD! The land of your inheritance is assured. My provision on your behalf is better than the vomit and vileness of your old life. It will be no honour to find yourself in the grave of your enemy. Shout in faith!

The call of my will is not to an office or self-seeking ambition. Joy becomes the property of those winners of the crown who have run the course to the very end.[36]

(W. Jones Williams)

Jot down anything you feel God might be saying to you personally.

_____

_____

_____

_____

_____

_____

Thank you God that you do not change, you are always faithful and because of this I can trust you completely. Your love does not falter, your promises to not shift and fly away – your nature and your covenant are unshakeable. You are a God who can fully be trusted. Amen.

---

[36] Prophet, W. Jones Williams, Penygroes, July 1926.

Day 26: This is war!

Further reading
Ephesians 6

Finally, my brethren, be strong in the Lord, and in the power of his might. Put on the whole armour of God, that ye may be able to stand against the wiles of the devil. Ephesians 6:10-11 (KJV)

What we have here is the warfare of the church, and the preparations God has made for his church, that she may come out victorious. There are a host of enemies trying to prevent the church of God from entering in to the purposes of God which are ahead. In order to go forward, the apostle commands us to "Be strong." It is a spiritual conflict, and it is only as we get spiritual strength that we are able to overcome in this terrible warfare. There is a sense in which we have to be a defensive church. Sometimes when the enemy attacks we can be wounded by him, and we have to return to the camp for healing, fresh courage and new equipment.[37]

(T. Vaughan Lewis)

Jot down anything you feel God might be saying to you personally.

_____

_____

_____

_____

_____

_____

Lord – thank you that you have given me everything I need to be victorious in the warfare of the church. Help me to be strong in Christ. Where I encounter wounds – help me to experience the healing of Christ. Amen.

---

[37] Apostle, T. Vaughan Lewis, July 1926.

Day 27: The Wine of Inspiration

Further reading
Proverbs 3

So shall thy barns be filled with plenty, and thy presses shall burst out with new wine. Proverbs 3:10 (KJV)

How often are we surprised when apparently fruitful lives are laid aside and the pressing begins! As it continues, it seems to end for many years the previous progress and growth; yet how often we have found afterwards that these same lives are full of bottled sunshine. It is natural for this to happen, we say, when man is making wine; but God would never do such a thing. But if God wants us to have the best wine in our midst, we must realise that he will only make it for use when we allow him to use the best methods. This gets the best results. And what glorious wine it will be – real sunshine that will open the fountains of joy in our midst. May God help us to see that The Lord's pressing is the opportunity for him to put sparkle and joy into our lives and that those who are dying by the roadside will be able to taste the wine of the kingdom that flows through us.[38]

(C. Dixon)

Jot down anything you feel God might be saying to you personally.

_____

_____

_____

_____

_____

_____

Lord, there are times when it seems like I'm undergoing a crushing. Thank you that pressing is not designed to destroy, but to produce new wine that will quench the thirst of all who are dry. Amen.

[38] Elder, C. Dixon, Bradford, 1926.

Day 28: A lesson from Doves

Further reading
2 Peter 1

For by these He has granted to us His precious and magnificent promises, so that by them you may become partakers of the divine nature, having escaped the corruption that is in the world by lust. 2 Peter 1:4 (NASB)

Doves have been a great object lesson to me. Although their dwelling place is the filthiest possible, yet they are the cleanest of all. Our Lord wants us to be like the dove. Although we live "in the world", we are called to be "not of the world." Whilst we travel on this pilgrimage through life, let us reflect the conduct, conversation and values of our "heavenly home." The dove has a shy, tender, beautiful, and royal nature which is far above the standard of her environment and surroundings. Although Jesus was called "the friend of sinners", his calling and nature still caused him to be eternally separate from them. The Holy Spirit also, whilst he is dwelling in his people, and even dealing with lost people through us, is eternally holy. We are in the world, but we are not of the world.[39]

(Henry Hughes Tumble)

Jot down anything you feel God might be saying to you personally.

_____

_____

_____

_____

_____

_____

Lord, thank you for the dove-like nature that you have given me through the new-birth. Amen.

---

[39] Elder Henry Hughes Tumble, quoted by F.C Bowen, 1926, Riches of Grace p55.

Day 29: When You Fail

Further reading
1 John 1

**For though the righteous fall seven times, they rise again.
Proverbs 24:16 (NIV)**

Don't break your heart if you fail in your objectives. Remember, even if you fail, you have "fallen on the hearth." A child falls many times before mastering the walk that is the delight of the household. If you fall, call out to your Father in Heaven. He will surely raise you up. [*Think about Peter's restoration.*][40] Peter's expression of speech beside the enemy's fire, so similar to the men of Galilee, only added to the grief of our Lord. But his speech following the [restoration and][41] silence of obedience, in line with the divine ordination, swept thousands into the kingdom at Pentecost, adding greatly to the exaltation of the Lord in the eyes of Israel.[42]

(Henry Hughes Tumble)

Jot down anything you feel God might be saying to you personally.

_____

_____

_____

_____

_____

_____

Thank you, Jesus, for amazing grace that picks me up when I fall. You never leave me or forsake me – even when I sin – your grace pursues me. Amen.

---

[40] Added by editor for clarification.

[41] Added by editor for clarification.

[42] Elder Henry Hughes Tumble, quoted by F.C Bowen, 1926, Riches of Grace p56.

Day 30: Ask for the Impossible

Further reading
Hebrews 11

After these things the word of the Lord came unto Abram in a vision, saying, Fear not, Abram: I am thy shield, and thy exceeding great reward. Genesis 15:1 (KJV)

God came so near now, and gave him (Abram) such a vision of his greatness and power; a personal knowledge; a personal revelation of God – that now his hopes were raised. He now prayed that God would give him a son. Now he had faith. He saw God in a new light, and he prayed for a son. Well, the Lord is going to give us such a revelation of his nature; we are going to see his kindness, his mercy, his love and care over us. He is going to give us faith to ask for great things – personal things, which is permitted when it is for his glory, but especially things for the advancement of his church.[43]

(Joseph Larkins)

Jot down anything you feel God might be saying to you personally.

_____

_____

_____

_____

_____

_____

Thank you, Lord God that you are a great and mighty God and nothing is impossible for you. You have given me great and precious promises – help me to lay hold of your promises and by faith ask you for large God-honouring miracles – increase my capacity to believe you for great things. Amen.

---

[43] Apostle Joseph Larkins, USA, 1926.

Day 31: Unity: Soar Higher

Further reading
Galatians 3

There is neither Jew nor Greek, there is neither slave nor free man, there is neither male nor female; for you are all one in Christ Jesus. Galatians 3:28 (NASB)

Airmen tell us that the first experience they have as they are ascending is that they lose sight of the hedges between fields. As they climb higher, they lose the distinction between town and country. Yet higher still, the distinction between land and sea is gone. One wide expanse fills the vision. The higher we are in him, the more we shall be able to echo the words of Paul, "There is neither Greek nor Jew... but Christ is all in all."

The evil one attempts to divide the church through divisions and false teachings. The Holy Spirit always leads to unity. He cannot be restricted to a corner or to a nation, or to a certain class of people.[44]

(William H. Lewis)

Jot down anything you feel God might be saying to you personally.

_____

_____

_____

_____

_____

_____

Lord, let us rise higher until all distinctions are gone, and all we see is Christ. Thank you for the glorious truth that the higher we ascend in the Spirit, the less division we see – take us higher that we may be One. Amen.

---

[44] Apostle, William H. Lewis, Penygroes, 1934.

Day 32: The New Birth

Further reading
John 3

Jesus answered and said to him, "Truly, truly, I say to you, unless one is born [a]again he cannot see the kingdom of God." John 3:3 (NASB)

We hear much today about the popular teaching of the universal Fatherhood of God and the global unity of humanity. The outcome is that the distinction between the regenerate (those who are born again) and the unregenerate (those who are not born again) is obliterated. Regeneration (New Birth) is imperative. The New Birth is a foundational truth of the gospel.

To be made partakers of the Divine Nature is the glorious news of the gospel. "If anyone is in Christ he is a new creation": A new creation, new desires, a new experience, and a new outlook transform the believer.[45]

(William H. Lewis)

Jot down anything you feel God might be saying to you personally.

_____

_____

_____

_____

_____

_____

Thank you, Father, for the new birth. Were it not for the work of your Spirit in my heart, I'd still be dead in sin, blind to your glory, and held captive by chains. Thank you for the power of new life – I am a new creation in Christ, old things have gone – all things are being made new! Amen.

---

[45] Apostle, William H. Lewis, Penygroes, 1934.

Day 33: Transformed (Part 1)

Further reading
Exodus 40

And Moses was not able to enter into the tent of the congregation, because the cloud abode thereon, and the glory of the Lord filled the tabernacle. Exodus 40: 35 (KJV)

Vision must be substantiated by a living experience. It is not enough to be enlightened. It is possible to have a mental vision of the church of the New Testament in its glorious principles, ministries and callings, and yet be destitute of divine power. Moses' Tabernacle, although constructed minutely after the Divine Pattern, was an empty tent and a meaningless structure until the glory overshadowed and filled its courts. Solomon's Temple was only a magnificent edifice, pleasing to the eye, and a masterpiece of human workmanship, until the cloud of glory filled the spacious courts, and the grandeur of man was buried in the excelling glory of God's presence.[46]

(William H. Lewis)

Jot down anything you feel God might be saying to you personally.

_____

_____

_____

_____

_____

_____

Lord, no matter how many gifts I have, no matter how much experience I have, and no matter the kind of skills I have – without your glory anointing my life, it is all just a work of the flesh. Fill me with your glory. Amen.

---

[46] Apostle, William H. Lewis, Penygroes, 1934.

Day 34: Transformed (Part 2)

Further reading
Acts 4

Now when they saw the boldness of Peter and John, and perceived that they were unlearned and ignorant men, they marvelled; and they took knowledge of them, that they had been with Jesus. Acts 4:13 (KJV)

The outpouring of the Holy Spirit on the Day of Pentecost turned those poor insignificant fishermen into a living host vibrant with life, vision and power. They kicked off a new era in the face of relentless enemies, and cruel opposition. We need to partake more deeply of the life of God. We need a renewed vision – the pattern from the Mount. We have it! We need a fresh endowment of power and to realise anew the weight of glory that has been committed to us by Christ, the glory of the ripened and redeeming predestined purposes of God for these days![47]

(William H. Lewis)

Jot down anything you feel God might be saying to you personally.

_____

_____

_____

_____

_____

_____

O God of burning cleansing flame: Send the fire!
Your blood-bought gift today we claim: Send the fire today! Look down and see this waiting host,
And send the promised Holy Ghost; We need another Pentecost! Send the fire today![48]

---

[47] Apostle, William H. Lewis, Penygroes, 1934.

[48] Hymn by William Booth.

Day 35: Transformed (Part 3)

Further reading
1 Samuel 1

For this ...I prayed; and the Lord hath given me my petition which I asked of him. 1 Samuel: 1:27 (KJV)

Prayer will bring us closer fellowship with the yearning heart of Christ who prayed and died that his scattered sheep might be brought into the One Fold and under the One Great Shepherd. We also trust the solemn responsibility placed upon us as we are passing over to a New Testament era with an enriched and inspired God-given vision to meet the increasing demands of the church. God will stir our hearts afresh, and cause us to dedicate ourselves on the altar of consecration. We are confident of this, that if we will seize this unparalleled opportunity to respond to the momentous call of God to us as his people at this time, the fire will fall and Zion will be ablaze with a heavenly visitation.[49]

(William H. Lewis)

Jot down anything you feel God might be saying to you personally.

_____

_____

_____

_____

_____

_____

_____

Precious Lord, as I meditate on the words of your servants from yester-year, I am challenged by their zeal and their depth. Help me to know you as intimately. Help me to seek you with all of my heart. Help me surrender all that I am to you –please take over my life and be Lord of all.
In Jesus' name, Amen.

---

[49] Apostle, William H. Lewis, Penygroes, 1934.

Day 36: More

Further reading
1 Thess. 5

And the very God of peace sanctify you wholly; and I pray God your whole spirit and soul and body be preserved blameless unto the coming of our Lord Jesus Christ. 1 Thessalonians 5:23 (KJV)

Some of us know the blessing of sanctification, but the Lord is able to give you so much more than this. Do not stop at the blessing. The Lord is able to give you much more purity of heart; purity of intent and motive until your whole being is cleansed by God. God can work in your heart to the point where you cannot bear to think evil of anyone. That is true sanctification.

He is also able to give you more passion for souls. There are people perishing all around us, carried away by a flood of sin, and we know of Christ's power, and the blood that is able to cleanse and save them. Lord God! Give us a passion for souls, that the burden and its passion may become unbearable.[50]

(T. Rees)

Jot down anything you feel God might be saying to you personally.

_____

_____

_____

_____

_____

_____

Lord, thank you there's always more with you. I can't ever exhaust your fullness. Forgive me for settling for scraps, when you provide a feast. Amen.

---

[50] Apostle, T. Rees, 1931, Pontypridd.

Day 37: Abiding in Him

Further reading
John 15

If ye abide in me, and my words abide in you, ye shall ask what ye will, and it shall be done unto you. John 15:7 (KJV)

Abiding in Christ affects our prayer life. What wonderful possibilities are within this promise! The world is full of unanswered prayers, and we are blaming all sorts of things for this: hardness of people's hearts, environment and different circumstances. But, beloved – here is a promise that is ABOVE EVERY CIRCUMSTANCE! The promise states clearly, "If you abide" it shall be done! Unsaved friends and others we don't know will be saved. Empty churches will be filled. And many mighty miracles and signs will manifest once we have solved the problem of this wonderful life of abiding in him.[51]

(J Lindsay)

Jot down anything you feel God might be saying to you personally.

_____

_____

_____

_____

_____

_____

Thank you, Father, for this great and awesome promise. I confess that I barely scratch the surface of all that is available to me in Christ. Help me to abide and help me discover the assurance of answered prayers which flow from this union. Amen.

---

[51] Apostle, J. Lindsay, Edinburgh, 1931.

Day 38: Pray and Give Thanks

Further reading
2 Thess. 2

**But we are bound to give thanks always to God for you, brethren beloved of the Lord
2 Thessalonians 2:13 (KJV)**

If we were to thank God more for one another, perhaps we would pray more for one another. Whatever our failures and short comings, we can thank God for one thing. When you think of some believer, and say, "Thank God for him (or her)" you will feel something burning in your heart for him. The result will be that you will pray for him. But the danger is that we criticise one another and watch one another and we talk about one another. The result of that is we cannot pray for one another. Show me someone who is judging another person, and I'll show you someone who is not praying for that person. If you want a good ministry, pray for your leaders.[52]

(T.V. Lewis)

Jot down anything you feel God might be saying to you personally.

_____

_____

_____

_____

_____

_____

Father, help me to give thanks for everyone in my life – when I am tempted to criticise, help me to give thanks and when I have given thanks – help me to intercede. Amen.

---

[52] Apostle, T.V. Lewis, 1931, Skewan.

Day 39: Breathe

Further reading
2 Thess. 3

Finally, brethren, pray for us. 2 Thessalonians 3:1 (KJV)

The highest effort in the Christian life, no doubt, is prayer. And it is so because it is the first expression of the Christian life. The most essential thing in your natural life is that you breathe. The moment you fail to breathe, you are done with. So the most important thing in our lives is that we pray, that we breathe well. Deep breathing. Breathing that will take God down deep into the depth of our being – not short breathings. Our lungs are not very good, and we are not as strong as we ought to be. If we are not people of prayer, the danger is that our lungs become congested, because our life is not in God.[53]

(T.V. Lewis)

Jot down anything you feel God might be saying to you personally.

_____

_____

_____

_____

_____

_____

Breath of God – come fill my lungs with the Father's pure presence. Fill my spirit with the Spirit of Christ. Help me breathe deeply the fresh air of heaven. Help me to breathe long, deep, and satisfying breaths. Help me to breathe regularly, and in in step with the rhythm of heaven. Amen.

---

[53] Apostle, T.V. Lewis, 1931, Skewan.

Day 40: Holiness and Purity

Further reading
Hebrews 12

Follow peace with all men, and holiness, without which no man shall see the Lord. Hebrews 12:14 (KJV)

Come near, and I will purify you. I will cause holiness to be within. There can be no outward manifestation of holiness unless it is within. Has the Word worked within you? Many of you are studying the works of men. The study is good, if the men are good, for good can only come from good. But you must study my word. Are you holy? Are you pure? You cannot proclaim holiness and purity, if you are not. You must possess – then you shall hear! Forsake the sins that are hindering you. Seek after purity, and I the Lord will be honoured.[54]

(J. Omri Jones)

Jot down anything you feel God might be saying to you personally.

_____

_____

_____

_____

_____

_____

Purify my life oh Lord. Sanctify every part of me. Cleanse my heart, soul, mind and body of anything that contaminates. Cleanse me afresh by the blood of Jesus Christ. Renew me by your Spirit. Help me cut off everything that hinders and grieves your Spirit. In Jesus' Name: Amen.

---

[54] Pastor, J. Omri Jones, 1931, Ammanford.

Day 41: Invisible made Visible

Further reading
Romans 4

As it is written, "I have made you the father of many nations"— in the presence of the God in whom he believed, who gives life to the dead and calls into existence the things that do not exist. Romans 4:17 (ESV)

My word does not go forward in vain. I am moving and bringing into being that which is invisible and hidden to the eyes of men and women. I AM GOING TO DECLARE, NOT IN WORD ONLY, BUT IN A DEMONSTRATION OF POWER AND LIGHT THAT I AM NOT ONLY ABLE TO CONTROL THE INVISIBLE BUT THE VISIBLE ALSO. *IF* YOU WILL SURRENDER within your heart to the movements of my Spirit, your heart will also be opened for that which I am accomplishing in the visible. Do not let "unity" be declared as something invisible only, it MUST become visible.[55]

(Interpretation of tongues)

Jot down anything you feel God might be saying to you personally.

_____

_____

_____

_____

_____

_____

Lord, thank you that you desire to manifest that which is in heaven on earth. You desire to bring the unseen into the realm of the seen. Lord, let me be a conduit where heaven flows to earth and that which is invisible becomes visible.
Amen.

---

[55] Interpretation of tongues, 6th August, 1934.

Day 42: Take Courage

Further reading
Joshua 1

Have I not commanded you? Be strong and courageous. Do not be afraid; do not be discouraged, for the LORD your God will be with you wherever you go." Joshua 1:9 (NIV)

Be of good courage my people, for I can still play the harp, for I am able to play upon the words of truth that are given in my word. I am speaking of divine revelation, and I am saying: "As my people, be of good courage!" It is the positive side I desire to bring to you, in order that your eyes may be opened to the truth that the people of God are moving on! Be of good courage, I am still your leader, your God. I am still the Captain of your Salvation. I am still in front of my word and I am declaring: The church of God is marching on! Whatever you feel, whatever you think, whatever your idea is about these things, I am declaring from my throne: the church of God is marching on! Remember that I am bringing my church to perfection. Satan will attempt to frustrate the plans I have in view, but I have declared that the gates of hell shall not prevail against my church! [56]

(T. Napier Turnbull)

Jot down anything you feel God might be saying to you personally.

_____

_____

_____

_____

_____

_____

Lord, thank you that I can be strong in you.
Amen.

---

[56] T. Napier Turnbull, Prophetic Ministry, 1934.

Day 43: Deliverance

Further reading
2 Kings 17

"But the LORD your God you shall fear; and He will deliver you from the hand of all your enemies." 2 Kings 17:39 (NASB)

I have given you faith that will cause you to realise all the divine mysteries and to know that the will of God is being accomplished. Have I not delivered you in the past? Have you not proven that in the midst of troubles and difficulties that I have delivered you? Can you declare it, my people? I HAVE DELIVERED YOU! Realise now that I am delivering you – all the time. My hand is delivering, and surely I HAVE delivered you, and I AM delivering you! You can surely rejoice in the fact that I WILL deliver you. Here is your salvation: in the realisation that what your God *has* done, and what I *am* doing, and what I *will* do again. I am Almighty. I am able to deliver. There is NONE like me. I am a Man of War. I have declared it in my word. I want the realisation of these things to grip your soul.[57]

(T. Napier Turnbull)

Jot down anything you feel God might be saying to you personally.

_____

_____

_____

_____

_____

_____

Thank you Lord that you are mighty in battle. I praise you because you HAVE delivered me, you ARE delivering me, and you WILL deliver me! Amen.

---

[57] T. Napier Turnbull, Prophetic Ministry, 1934.

Day 44: My Presence

Further reading
Psalm 103

The LORD replied, "My Presence will go with you, and I will give you rest." Exodus 33:14 (NIV)

How do you feel in my presence? My delight is with the people I have created. There is no language that can convey to you in a fuller measure and sense my thoughts, my feelings, my desire, and my love towards people. My desires are always towards the people I have made in my image. If this is true, then be comfortable in my presence. Know that I am the Lord who heals you. I cannot but heal. This is my function. I desire for my presence to be so real. How do you feel in my presence? How has my presence affected you? Do you believe in the light of my word: the expression of my will to heal? Let the welcome and warmth of my love embrace and possess you.[58]

(W.J. Williams)

Jot down anything you feel God might be saying to you personally.

_____

_____

_____

_____

_____

_____

Father thank you for your presence and that you made us for fellowship with you. We were designed for intimacy. Help me to rest in your presence at all times. In Jesus' Name, Amen.

---

[58] W.J. Williams, Prophetic Ministry, 1934.

Day 45: Born to a Higher Life

Further reading
Psalm 1

We exhorted each one of you and encouraged you and charged you to walk in a manner worthy of God, who calls you into his own kingdom and glory. 1 Thessalonians 2:12 (ESV)

When a person is born again into the kingdom, follows the royal command to be baptised in water, and is sealed by the baptism of the Holy Spirit, he stands in relationship, first to the risen Lord, as head of the body, the church. Secondly, to all those that are members by operation of the Holy Spirit, and have heard the call of God out of all that is detrimental and disadvantageous to spiritual fellowship and growth. The church is the called out body of believers, but called in by God to himself and for himself. It is a stripping off and a cutting away from all connections, relations and affairs of this life which in any way prevent (by entanglements) the soul from making a complete surrender to the will of God. The truly repentant person abandons himself to God, to be possessed by the power and resources of a higher realm.[59]

(D.P. Williams)

Jot down anything you feel God might be saying to you personally.

_____

_____

_____

_____

_____

_____

Lord Jesus, thank you for the new birth – help me surrender every area of my life to you. Amen.

[59] D.P. Williams, 1934.

65

Day 46: Perils of the Victorious Life (Part 1)

Further reading
2 Cor.11

No wonder, for even Satan disguises himself as an angel of light. 2 Corinthians 11:14 (NASB)

The very joy of the yielded life, when God's will is wholly accepted, brings with it another danger. When Satan discovers he cannot prevent you from doing the whole will of God, he will try to drive you *beyond* the will of God. And it is a dangerous thing to go beyond the will of God, even in matters that of themselves are good and right. Satan will seek to drive you towards imaginary duties. (He appears as an angel of light). He will suggest that you should do this or that good thing – but although it is good, it is not God's will for you. You know how greatly blessed you have been when you have followed the voice of the Spirit and instantly obeyed his leadings. Satan may also prompt believers to do something 'good' but instead of blessing following the action there is only anxiety, confusion, doubt and fog.[60]

(Charles Gallandet Trumbull)

Jot down anything you feel God might be saying to you personally.

_____

_____

_____

_____

_____

_____

Lord, help me never to go beyond your will. Enable me to discern the difference between your leading, the desires of my own flesh, and the distractions of the enemy.

---

[60] Charles Gallandet Trumbull, 1934.

Day 47: Perils of the Victorious Life (Part 2)

Further reading
Ecc. 3

There is a time for everything, and a season for every activity under the heavens. Ecclesiastes 3:1 (NIV)

The victorious life is a supernatural life. It is a living miracle, a thrilling adventure because it is God's work and God's working. Our early experiences in the life of victory are likely to be so different from anything we have known before, so out of the ordinary in supernatural demonstration of God's grace and power, that at once we are plunged into a peril. That peril is that we mistakenly assume that we must continually be having thrilling, unexpected supernatural evidences of God's power. And if these supernatural phenomena do not occur, we are tempted to think that something is wrong.

Now God wants us to trust, not in supernatural experiences, but in Him. It is for him to decide when the unusual happens or when our life should be 'ordinary' (so far as sight and sense are concerned). It is safe for us to assume that the "supernatural" (where our experiences are concerned) should be unusual events rather than usual events in the life of believers.[61]

(Charles Gallandet Trumbull)

Jot down anything you feel God might be saying to you personally.

_____

_____

_____

_____

_____

_____

In miracles or mundaneness, I will praise you.

---

[61] Charles Gallandet Trumbull, 1934.

Day 48: Perils of the Victorious Life (Part 3)

Further reading
1 Cor. 13

**Now our knowledge is partial and incomplete, and even the gift of prophecy reveals only part of the whole picture!
1 Corinthians 13:9 (NLT)**

Let us be delivered from the danger of assuming an infallible knowledge of God's will. God's leadings may be so blessed, and unmistakable that, as we testify to others about them, we say, "God said this to me," or "God led me to do that." And then, if we are not on our guard, we thoughtlessly slip into habitual expressions about God's telling us what to do, and God's leading us. Some Christians almost never speak of any action or decision of theirs without prefacing it with the words that God told them to do this or that. And quite often in the experience of such a one, later circumstances show plainly that God did not tell them to do this, or that, but that they had misunderstood his leading, as is possible at any time for any believer, even while wholly yielded. Instead of saying "God told me," is it not better to say, "I believe God would have me do this,"? Let us recognise we may be mistaken, even if we are quite certain in our hearts.[62]

(Charles Gallandet Trumbull)

Jot down anything you feel God might be saying to you personally.

_____

_____

_____

_____

_____

_____

Lord, keep me hearing, keep me humble

---

[62] Charles Gallandet Trumbull, 1934.

Day 49: Perils of the Victorious Life (Part 4)

Further reading
1 John 5

Who is the one who overcomes the world, but he who believes that Jesus is the Son of God? 1 John 5:5 (NASB)

The secret of complete victory is faith: simply believing that *Jesus has done, and is doing it all.* Victory is received as a simple act of faith – as is salvation. Victory is maintained by the attitude of faith. But suppose the believer, having experienced the miracle of victory over sin through trusting his Lord's sufficiency, comes, somehow to doubt that sufficiency? At once his victory is broken and he fails. This is possible at any moment. And at once, if there should be failure through unbelief, there comes a real danger. The lie of Satan whispers in the ear. He tells us we have sinned and never had the victory.

They say at Keswick "If you should fail, shout victory!" Not with the idea of denying the reality of the failure, but in recognition of the fact that Jesus has not failed and that there may be instantaneous and complete restoration through faith in his unimpaired sufficiency.[63]

(Charles Gallandet Trumbull)

Jot down anything you feel God might be saying to you personally.

_____

_____

_____

_____

_____

_____

Thank you Jesus for VICTORY OVER EVERY OBSTACLE.

---

[63] Charles Gallandet Trumbull, 1934.

69

Day 50: Divine Overfamiliarity

Further reading
Numbers 11

But now we have lost our appetite; we never see anything but this manna!" Numbers 11:6 (NIV)

We are often reminded in these days of the danger of becoming familiar with the things of God. The warning especially applies to the ministry of the spoken word. "Custom doth make it to become unto us a matter of easiness." The extent of the value placed upon the word must always be viewed in the light of its source, and in the benefit obtained when its application affects our lives. The Lord has been reminding us that we have lost the sanctity, reverence and honour of things pertaining to him. It may be that the weight of the words is minimised because we fail to meditate upon them, and neglect to apply them to our lives.[64]

(Cyril Mathews)

Jot down anything you feel God might be saying to you personally.

_____

_____

_____

_____

_____

_____

Lord God Almighty, forgive me for becoming overfamiliar with your presence, your word and your purposes. Help me stay fresh in my love for you.

---

[64] Pastor, Cyril Mathews, Glasgow, 1934.

Day 51: A Baptism of Fire

Further reading
Mark 1

I baptize you with water, but he will baptize you with the Holy Spirit." Mark 1:8 (NIV)

We may be in danger of neglecting the great need of a further visitation. We may be guilty of lowering the standard of conditions, endeavoring to get the people through a superficial evidence of the baptism of fire. Some of us will never forget the humbling, stripping and breaking-up time that we experienced under the Spirit's visitation when the soil of our natural self was prepared for the rain of heaven. Think of the term we use, "Baptism **in** the Spirit," which conveys the thought of immersion, ("burial"), as when one is buried in the baptism of water, bodily. Does it not mean that the soul is experimentally passing through death, and buried in the divine, floods of divine life, power and fire permeating the whole of our being, bringing the sense of sanctity, and of purification, the tranquility of heavenly peace, radiating the consciousness?[65]

(D.P. Williams)

Jot down anything you feel God might be saying to you personally.

_____

_____

_____

_____

_____

_____

Lord, forgive me for diluting the reality of what it means to be baptised in your Holy Spirit. Pentecost is not a little splash of water on the head; it is a complete immersion into the heart of the Triune God – an encounter with all-consuming fire.

---

[65] Apostle, D.P. Williams, 1934.

Day 52: Led by the Spirit

Further reading
Luke 4

And Jesus, full of the Holy Spirit, returned from the Jordan and was led by the Spirit in the wilderness. Luke 4:1 (ESV)

And Jesus returned in the power of the Spirit to Galilee, and a report about him went out through all the surrounding country. Luke 4:14 (ESV)

This indwelling of the Holy Spirit works deeper than feelings in the source of our life, for it should mould the will, form our character, inspire us with new purposes, and illuminate the soul with heavenly vision. Spiritual wisdom, understanding and knowledge, come with the growth of the spiritual man. Growth, however, is conditional. The overflowing ministry of our Lord was led and dominated by the Spirit. We must be prepared for the Spirit to lead us along the path of life, the wilderness being the training ground.[66]

(D.P. Williams)

Jot down anything you feel God might be saying to you personally.

_____

_____

_____

_____

_____

_____

Father, thank you for filling me with your Holy Spirit, I pray that you will help me to yield to his work in order that the power of the Holy Spirit and the character of Christ will be seen in me more fully.

---

[66] Apostle, D.P. Williams, 1934.

Day 53: The Fountain of Life

Further reading
John 14

In that day you will know that I am in my Father, and you in me, and I in you. John 14:20 (ESV)

And God has given us his Spirit as proof that we live in him and he in us. John 4:13 (NLT)

The question often arises in your hearts, my people, "Why were we created? What is the purpose of life?" I will answer your questions. The answer to the questions surrounding the relationship between God and people are recorded in my word. The cravings, the desires, and the yearnings of your hearts can only be fulfilled and satisfied in me. You work, but you don't know why. You struggle with questions, but get no answers. Here is the solution to the problem: I am the fountain of life. The height, depth, breadth, and length of your calling is vastly more tremendous than you have previously thought or considered it. People are created in the image of God, after our likeness – there is within each of you a habitation for the Triune God – Father, Son and Holy Spirit.[67]

(Thomas Turnbull)

Jot down anything you feel God might be saying to you personally.

_____

_____

_____

_____

_____

_____

Lord you will not settle for a visitation, you desire habitation – make me a dwelling place for your Glory!

---

[67] Prophet, Thomas Turnbull, 1927.

Day 54: Turn from Idols

Further reading
2 Peter 3

For they keep talking about the wonderful welcome you gave us and how you turned away from idols to serve the living and true God. 1 Thessalonians 1:9 (NLT)

Truly the Lord says to you: does not your joy, does not your rejoicing consist in this, that you have turned from idols to me, the Living God, and you have left the idols behind, and you are no longer slaves to sin? As you rejoice in me, you are given power, and when you are engaged in serving me, your eyes are upward turned. There is a day coming when the veil that separates shall be removed. And although you now rejoice, seeing me by faith, then you shall see me face to face. My return draws near. Can you truly say you have turned to me, and have forsaken all idols? You cannot abide and live with me, if there are any idols clinging to you. I would have you to be in the position where your hope is brightened, and in the power and strength of that hope, you may be purified, ready and clothed for that day.[68]

(J. Omri Jones)

Jot down anything you feel God might be saying to you personally.

_____

_____

_____

_____

_____

_____

Lord, search me, strip away all things that captivate my heart and seduce me away from loving you whole-heartedly.

---

[68] Prophet, J. Omri Jones, 1927.

Day 55: Solace from the Sanctuary (Part 1)

Further reading
John 15

In that day you will know that I am in my Father, and you in me, Let him kiss me with the kisses of his mouth-- for your love is more delightful than wine. Song of Solomon 1:2 (NIV)

What precious truth does the Holy Spirit desire to teach us through this beautiful passage? What are "the kisses of his mouth"? Are they not the very words that come from the lips of the Lord Jesus Christ during his ministry on earth, especially at the time he endeavoured to comfort his disciples just before his crucifixion? (Read John chapters 14-16). When frightened, hurt or unable to understand things, a little child will run to its mother seeking comfort and consolation, and the mother will pick up the little one in her arms and charm away its sorrows with kisses and caresses. Similarly, when we find ominous clouds gathering and the risen life losing its flavour, we seek the uplifting presence of Jesus, desiring him to restore to us peace and joy of salvation by imparting to us "the kisses of his mouth."[69]

(Cyril H. Maskrey)

Jot down anything you feel God might be saying to you personally.

_____

_____

_____

_____

_____

_____

Restore me Oh Lord and I shall be restored. Rekindle the flames of my first love.

---

[69] Overseer, Cyril H. Maskrey, Scotland, 1927.

Day 56: Solace from the Sanctuary (Part 2)

Further reading
John 16

Let him kiss me with the kisses of his mouth! For your love is better than wine. (ESV)

The secret of being able to obtain and relish the manifold blessings of God lies in the first word of the text, "LET". If indeed we feel like empty barrels, we must remove any obstructing "lid" to allow the blessings to be poured into us. With vigilant and ever-watchful eye, the Good Shepherd sees when one of his flock is in distress, and it his delight to be able to take that one in his arms and say, "Let not your heart be troubled." (John 14:1) What a wonderful soothing influence are in these simple words – the kisses of His mouth! Joy has gone from our heart, Satan has put a cloud in the way, and the vision of the future – the coming of the Lord, is obscured and our troubled heart seeks for a ray of sunshine. Oh how these words from the lips of Jesus thrill the heart and cause renewed rejoicing in our glorious hope.[70]

(Cyril H. Maskrey)

Jot down anything you feel God might be saying to you personally.

_____

_____

_____

_____

_____

_____

Thank you Lord for your comfort and peace. Stir my heart afresh to hope in you fully. Fill me with joy.

---

[70] Overseer, Cyril H. Maskrey, Scotland, 1927.

Day 57: Solace from the Sanctuary (Part 3)

Further reading
Song. 1

Kiss me—full on the mouth! Yes! For your love is better than wine. Song of Solomon 1:2 (MSG)

When we experience trials and tribulations, and winds of adversity ruffle the calmness of heart and mind, there is one who draws near with compassion and understanding, and from his lips flows the balm that soothes and softens. There are times we feel overwhelmed by the attacks of the enemy. The heart that revelled in the abiding love of Jesus begins to palpitate with anxiety and fear, and all the comfort of that love seems to have departed. Possessing the Comforter is the remedy, and if our harassed heart will seek the Lord Jesus, solace will soon be forth coming: "I will not leave you comfortless." (John 14:18) Child of God, seek for a closer intimacy with the Lord and the bliss and ecstasy resulting from such a blessed communion will find its expression in the words of the psalmist: "Righteousness and Peace have kissed each other." (Psalm 85:10)[71]

(Cyril H. Maskrey)

Jot down anything you feel God might be saying to you personally.

_____

_____

_____

_____

_____

_____

Draw me close Lord Jesus – keep me near the cross, may I sense the nearness of your touch.

---

[71] Overseer, Cyril H. Maskrey, Scotland, 1927.

Day 58: A Divine Environment

Further reading
Psalm 139

In him we live and move and have our being. Acts 17:28 (ESV)

The Lord is still round about his people. The presence of the Almighty one presses from the outward to the centre of your heart. You often say that you can't live apart from your environment. But the Lord desires to create the environment, where the atmosphere of the eternal will be so clear and piercing. The work in your heart will not just be temporal, but for the age to come. Because the Lord is round about you, let the thought penetrate your heart that the Lord is your environment. His presence, his life, and the illumination of his word encircles you, so that you may hear things that are genuinely divine. The Lord longs to be the environment of your whole life, so that everything within you will be attuned to the Divine Presence, that holiness may be found within you, and holiness may be found around you.[72]

(J.D. Eyenon)

Jot down anything you feel God might be saying to you personally.

_____

_____

_____

_____

_____

_____

Thank you Lord that you are the air I breathe – help me to breathe in deep breaths of your love and holiness!

---

[72] Pastor, J.D.Eyenon, 1931, Interpretation of tongues.

Day 59: Healing and Deliverance

Further reading
Isaiah 61

He has sent me to bind up the brokenhearted, to proclaim liberty to the captives. Isaiah 61 (ESV)

While undergoing a very serious operation, I caught a cough in my chest while lying on the operating table, which gave me 16 years of torment. I then underwent another operation in May 1926, and through this cough, I nearly lost my life, and was told if I came back again it would mean my death. This cough was most manifest at the Breaking of Bread service, which disturbed the congregation, especially going through the scenes of Calvary. Realising it was a demon, I went one Wednesday night to the Airdrie Assembly and through the ministry of pastor Turnbull, I was set free and have never been tormented since.[73]

(Sister Gallraith)

Jot down anything you feel God might be saying to you personally.

_____

_____

_____

_____

_____

_____

Lord give me discernment that I may know the difference between physical affliction, and spiritual affliction. Thank you for the authority I have in Christ. Teach me to walk in that victory.

---

[73] A testimony by Sister Gallraith, Motherwell, 1931.

Day 60: To the Backslider

Further reading
Luke 15

I will go home to my father and say, "Father, I have sinned against both heaven and you. Luke 15:18 (NLT)

We like to announce salvation for the sinner, but I think we should also remember the backslider. Many have gone away from God. Different things have driven them away from him. But thank God for a way back! The result of backsliding is seen on your face. Where is the glory that was once in your life? It has vanished away, sin has sent it out of your being. You have become weak, frail having gone away from God – but if you will bring yourself back to God, it will return. Sin has terrible consequences. The enemy wants your soul. The cloud may be black and dark, but as Moses was called into the dark cloud, God was there, and so we need to find God in the cloud. Thank God for a way to return. We read that the prodigal "arose." *Arise* and return to your father and your home![74]

(W. Grabham)

Jot down anything you feel God might be saying to you personally.

_____

_____

_____

_____

_____

_____

Amazing grace, how sweet the sound, that saved a wretch like me – thank you Jesus!

---

[74] Evangelist, W. Grabham, Belfast, 1931.

Day 61: Not by might, nor by power

Further reading
Zechariah 4

Then he said to me, "This is the word of the LORD to Zerubbabel saying, 'Not by might nor by power, but by My Spirit,' says the LORD of hosts. Zechariah 4:6 (NASB)

There is a danger, because we are gifted, for us to forget that we are dependent upon the Spirit of God to carry on the work. On the other hand, there is a danger, because of the claims of God, and the "Go"s of God, and the doors that are opening, and the mountains of obstacles that are climbing so high (especially for those called to nations overseas), staggering and frightening us to become despondent, but praise God, we have an encouraging word that it is not by might or power of man but "by my Spirit."[75]

(Stephen Bowen)

Jot down anything you feel God might be saying to you personally.

_____

_____

_____

_____

_____

_____

Thank you Father that I don't have to fulfil your calling in my own strength – for this is impossible – thank you for the power of your Spirit!

---

[75] Pastor, Stephen Bowen, London 1932.

Day 62: Apostles Today

Further reading
1 Cor. 12

And God has placed in the church first of all apostles. 1 Corinthians 12:28 (NIV)

We have had the audacity to say that we believe in apostles, when there were only two or three amongst us, some years ago. It was a terrible fight to believe it. We were blinded by that tradition amongst us, as members of the chapels, that, "apostles were done away with at the beginning!" But the Holy Spirit is not done away with! And if God the Holy Spirit, and God the Father and God the Son, are One, unchangeable in their essence, surely there are apostles in the Trinity, there are prophets in the Trinity, there are evangelists in the Trinity, and all the Offices and the Gifts. The Holy Spirit has not been done away with. The Holy Spirit has not been robbed of these gifts.[76]

(T. Rees)

Jot down anything you feel God might be saying to you personally.

_____

_____

_____

_____

_____

_____

Thank you Lord that you never change. Thank you also that you give leadership gifts to the church to equip the church for works of service. Help me flow in my calling within your Body.

---

[76] Apostle T. Rees, 1934.

Day 63: Poison of Sin

Further reading
Romans 3

There is no one righteous, not even one. Romans 3:10 (NIV)

It is very important to have a deep conviction and realisation of the nature of sin and its evil effect on the soul. It is essential to understand sin if we are going to understand holiness. Sin is not something in our imagination, or something that is relegated to a certain class of people. Sin is a fact that is deep in the consciousness of every living soul. There is nothing surer than this. We are all ready to agree that there is something wrong with our own heart. The evidences of sin are seen around us with all its devastating effect on humanity. Most of the world's media, pouring forth floods of vice and impurity, are ugly because they are no longer channels of goodness, truth and beauty, but rather attest to the fact of sin and its hideousness. Sin is in the consciousness of all. Not just in our will or action, it is down in the source of our nature, controlling and dominating our whole being.[77]

(D.P. Williams)

Jot down anything you feel God might be saying to you personally.

_____

_____

_____

_____

_____

_____

Thank you Jesus that your cross is the answer to my sin – thank you not only for pardon, but for power over sin!

---

[77] Apostle, D.P. Williams 1935.

Day 64: Ministry of the Storm (Part 1)

Further reading
Mark 4:35-41

Suddenly, as they were crossing the lake, a ferocious tempest arose, with violent winds and waves that were crashing into the boat until it was all but swamped. Mark 4:37 (TPT)

I am leading and guiding you now, as you realise this you will be filled with joy because the storm will not be to your detriment. The storm will not hinder the plan of God. On the contrary, the storm will cause you to be what I want you to be. Storms produce character in the lives of the saints. My people, don't assume that the will of God will be accomplished without storms. Don't expect to arrive at the Haven of Rest without having storms in your lives, individually, as families, assemblies, and as the wider body of Christ. There are storms ahead, greater storms than you have experienced, I am only allowing the storms, as you are able to stand them. I am supplying the grace for the needed hour. The storm is good for you, whilst I send the storm, I supply the grace.[78]

(T. Napier Turnbull)

Jot down anything you feel God might be saying to you personally.

_____

_____

_____

_____

_____

_____

Thank you Jesus that you are with me in the storms and that the storms that come my way are leading me into your purposes.

---

[78] Prophet, T.Napier Turnbull, a prophetic word, 1934.

Day 65: Ministry of the Storm (Part 2)

Further reading
Psalm 46

God is our refuge and strength, a very present help in trouble. (Psalm 46:1) (ESV)

I allow storms to come to you, not to disturb, upset or alarm you. Nor do I send the storm just for you to cry to out to me so that I will calm the storm. No! I send the storm so that you will be established. The storms of life are only causing you to seek and to find me, and to let you know that I AM with you. The storms of life, more than anything else, will cause you to come nearer to me. Oh that you would realise that I am not designing the storms to destroy you, but to ground and produce character, and faith, and life in you...Rejoice in knowledge that when I am with you, you have nothing to fear. There is no need to worry that you will be swamped by the storm. You will not be swamped, you will be purified, grounded and I will produce character in you.[79]

(T. Napier Turnbull)

Jot down anything you feel God might be saying to you personally.

_____

_____

_____

_____

_____

_____

Thank you that these storms are not a sign of your absence, but they are a sign of your deep work in my life.

---

[79] Prophet, T.Napier Turnbull, a prophetic word, 1934.

Day 66: Suspicion of God

Further reading
1 John 4

Perfect love casts out fear. 1 John 4:18 (NKJV)

When you do not realise that I am with you, FEAR comes upon you, and fear becomes a snare. When fear is in your heart, you do not realise that I am your friend. Some of you think at the present time that I am acting as an enemy, but I would have you realise that I am your Heavenly Father. For when I was walking towards my disciples on the stormy waves they thought I was "a spirit" – an enemy. But I was the Lord who was there to help them. If fear is in your heart, you will think I am an enemy. But if faith is in your heart, when you are "of good courage" then you will realise that I am your friend. And I AM your friend![80]

(T. Napier Turnbull)

Jot down anything you feel God might be saying to you personally.

_____

_____

_____

_____

_____

_____

Father thank you that you love me. Help me rest in your love. Thank you that your love is the key that will help me live a fear-free life. Thank you that your love washes all my anxieties away. Thank you that I am loved and nothing can change this.

---

[80] Prophet, T.Napier Turnbull, a prophetic word, 1934.

Day 67: The Need: Calebs & Joshuas

Further reading
Numbers 13

Then Caleb quieted the people before Moses and said, "We should by all means go up and take possession of it, for we will surely overcome it." Numbers 13:30 (NASB)

I desire Calebs and Joshuas again! "Men of another Spirit." For there are too many who are dying in the wilderness. There are too many who are lagging behind, who have fear in their hearts. I desire you to be like Caleb and Joshua. Men of a different spirit, men of faith, men who have the courage to go in and possess the land. I will give you this courage, this faith. For I have spoken on the great things I have done. What did I do through Samson? One man slew a thousand. What did I do through David? I overcame the giant. The great things I have done in the past, I am able to do again. I am still the same as I was in the early days of the church. You have read in the Acts of the apostles what I have done through my apostles and prophets. Do you believe I can do the same today?[81]

(T. Napier Turnbull)

Jot down anything you feel God might be saying to you personally.

_____

_____

_____

_____

_____

_____

Lord, make me one who has a different spirit.

---

[81] Prophet, T.Napier Turnbull, a prophetic word, 1934.

Day 68: Special Epochs: Special Vessels

Further reading
Esther 4

For if you remain completely silent at this time, relief and deliverance will arise for the Jews from another place, but you and your father's house will perish. Yet who knows whether you have come to the kingdom for such a time as this?" Esther 4:14 (NKJV)

I am raising up servants for such a time as this. Can you believe it? I have had special times in history; I have raised up men and women "for such a time as this" in *your* time! But I am still saying, "Be of good courage!" I am raising *you* up "for such a time as this." It is truly a critical time: a time when you have to be alive to the situation. But I tell you, on the other hand, A TIME OF GREAT POSSIBILITIES! For there are many who desired in the Dark Ages to live in the day that you are living. For they have looked forward to the time of the visitation of God being revealed in all its glory and majesty, that the church, as it has been revealed in the past, might be revealed in all its glory again – and that is what I am doing.[82]

(T. Napier Turnbull)

Jot down anything you feel God might be saying to you personally.

_____

_____

_____

_____

_____

_____

Thank you God that you are on the move and that you are raising up your people to do mighty works in the land.

---

[82] Prophet, T.Napier Turnbull, a prophetic word, 1934.

Day 69: Listen to my Voice

Further reading
1 Kings 19

After the earthquake came a fire, but the Lord was not in the fire. And after the fire came a gentle whisper. 1 Kings 19:12 (NIV)

I declare to you that I can have many who will run here and there. I have many who will go on my word and be servants. BUT I CAN HAVE FEW WHO LISTEN TO ME. TO HEAR THE BRIDEGROOM'S VOICE. I CAN HAVE MANY "Marthas" but few "Marys". I am looking for "Marys" in these days who will listen to my voice, and sit at my feet, and hear of me. It is they who are going to be greater servants in the end. Those who, in the prison, or the deepest dungeon, sit at my feet, and receive divine revelation. They in the end will be known and realised as servants of God.[83]

(T. Napier Turnbull)

Jot down anything you feel God might be saying to you personally.

_____

_____

_____

_____

_____

_____

Father, forgive me when I spend more time ministering for you than ministering to you. You desire intimacy. You don't want your people to serve you at a distance. Let your voice not be a faint echo in my life. Let my spirit be receptive to your faintest whispers. Help me to know your voice.

---

[83] Prophet, T.Napier Turnbull, a prophetic word, 1934.

Day 70: Music in the Heart

Further reading
1 Samuel 16

Whenever the spirit from God came on Saul, David would take up his lyre and play. Then relief would come to Saul; he would feel better, and the evil spirit would leave him. 1 Samuel 16:23

I desire to produce music in your heart. I can give you that string in your heart. There are many strings within you, but here is another: I want to add to you the string of music: "Be of good courage!" My servant of old played upon the harp until the evil spirit left the servant who was listening. There are some of you who have let the spirit of doubt; unbelief and fear come upon you. But "Be of Good Courage!" I am playing upon your heart, so that every demon of doubt, and fear and unbelief, and everything that is not of me, may leave, that you may have faith to believe![84]

(T. Napier Turnbull)

Jot down anything you feel God might be saying to you personally.

_____

_____

_____

_____

_____

_____

Thank you Lord that you give me heavenly melodies that become weapons of warfare. Help me to raise a shout of hallelujah and see the darkness flee. I will not be silent – I will sing praise in the darkness – my praise will awaken the dawn.

---

[84] Prophet, T.Napier Turnbull, a prophetic word, 1934.

Day 71: Thawed by God's love

Further reading
Rev. 2:1-7

But I have this against you, that you have abandoned the love you had at first. Revelation 2:4 (ESV)

Will you allow me to enfold and embrace you in this season? I want to warm your heart. There are external forces which make you cold: the spreading of lies, the spreading of untruths, the listening to and believing the whisperings of the father of lies. Why do you do this? Why give your ears to that which affects you negatively? Unbelief has been knocking at your heart's door, and lies and whisperings have affected your innermost being, until there is a coldness invading and possessing you. But let my word reach your innermost being, and I will cause the freezing to thaw, that you may know something of the eternal temperature of the Infinite Heart of Love, which is still towards you.[85]

(W. Jones Williams)

Jot down anything you feel God might be saying to you personally.

_____

_____

_____

_____

_____

_____

Melt my heart, Oh Lord. Soften it with your grace. Let my love not grow cold. Forgive me for letting the things of this world bring coldness into my spirit. Let me feel the warmth of your love in my spirit once again.

---

[85] Pastor W. Jones Williams, 1937.

Day 72: The Return of Christ (Part 1)

Further reading
Mark 13

"At that time people will see the Son of Man coming in clouds with great power and glory. Mark 13:26 (NIV)

The crowning event of redemption is the second coming of our Lord Jesus Christ. Our redemption was really commenced when Christ procured it on the cross of Calvary, when he fully atoned for our sins, where he (the Lamb) died for us. Our redemption began there objectively. Whenever a person accepts the Lord Jesus, he is justified from all his sins. As he receives the Word of God, he is born of God. Redemption begins subjectively at that very moment. This is the work of sanctification, because sanctification is an act as well as a process that will take place continually until the Lord returns, and when he comes, that will be the crowning event of our redemption. It is when he will put his finishing touch upon us, our bodies will be glorified.[86]

(T. Rees)

Jot down anything you feel God might be saying to you personally.

_____

_____

_____

_____

_____

_____

Lord Jesus – help me stay awake and alert and ever-ready for your return. Help me to repent of every sin. Purify my whole being – body, soul and spirit. Let there be nothing hidden in my life that would bring shame if you were to return and it were to be brought into the light.

---

[86] Apostle, T. Rees, 1933.

Day 73: The Return of Christ (Part 2)

Further reading
Romans 8

For the creation was subjected to frustration, not by its own choice, but by the will of the one who subjected it, in hope that the creation itself will be liberated from its bondage to decay and brought into the freedom and glory of the children of God. Romans 8:20-21 (NIV)

The greatest fact in history is that Jesus Christ, the Lord of Glory has been in this world of ours. The most important fact of the present is that he is in heaven interceding for us. And the greatest prophesied event of the future is that he is coming again. He himself said, "I will come again." The angels said he would come again. The apostles said he was coming again. This earth is marching fast towards a crisis, nothing but Jesus' return will get it out of this mess. Why do we not plead for his return every time we hear the clock strike?[87]

(T. Rees)

Jot down anything you feel God might be saying to you personally.

_____

_____

_____

_____

_____

_____

Lord, let your Kingdom come, let your will be done! Thank you that one day you will return and all things shall be well. The glory of God shall cover the whole earth once again.

---

[87] Apostle, T. Rees, 1933.

Day 74: Followers

Further reading
John 1

The next day Jesus decided to leave for Galilee. Finding Philip, he said to him, "Follow me." John 1:43 (NIV)

A disciple is one who takes his Christianity from Christ, not from Christians. A disciple is one who is following to learn, and learning to follow. "To follow" in scripture means: "to go on habitually after"; "to pursue with diligence"; and "to cleave and adhere to". We must follow the Lord for a CLEARER VISION. We must follow him for a DEEPER KNOWLEDGE. We must follow him for GREATER SERVICE. A disciple is one who is conscious of a lack in his life, but (Praise God!) conscious of a divine supply to meet that lack. Consequently we follow on in faith, and do not give up in despair.[88]

(H.W. Ogilvie)

Jot down anything you feel God might be saying to you personally.

_____

_____

_____

_____

_____

_____

Lord, help me to be a true follower. I don't want to be religious. I don't want to be a hypocrite. I want to be a real follower of the Lord. Thank you Lord that even though I am weak, you have an infinite supply of grace.

---

[88] Pastor, H.W. Ogilvie, Leeds, 1939.

Day 75: A Great God

Further reading
Psalm 18

With you as my strength I can crush an enemy horde, advancing through every stronghold that stands in front of me. What a God you are! Your path for me has been perfect! Psalm 18:29-30 (TPT)

God is very great in the midst of his people. He is the high and lofty one, inhabiting eternity – great in power. It is good to know that God desires to give us this power to overcome and live the victorious life. Let us become conscious of his presence. He knows our weakness; he is not nursing, but pouring in strength to enable us to fight the good fight of faith. Smooth paths are not always safe. We may get careless. The rough road makes us cautious, prayerful and dependent upon God.[89]

(Mrs J. Cardwell)

Jot down anything you feel God might be saying to you personally.

_____

_____

_____

_____

_____

_____

An old hymn says, "Satan trembles when he sees, the weakest saint upon his knees." Thank you Lord, that you prepare my hands for war. You are the One who fights my battles – and you haven't lost a battle yet – nor will you ever lose a battle. You are undefeatable!

---

[89] 1939.

Day 76: A Glasgow woman's testimony

Further reading
Acts 16

One of those listening was a woman from the city of Thyatira named Lydia, a dealer in purple cloth. She was a worshiper of God. The Lord opened her heart to respond to Paul's message. Acts 16:14 (NIV)

Praise God for godly mothers. I'm sorry I did not follow the Lord sooner in life. The Lord called me to follow him, but I took in my hand the lamp of profession, but with no oil. This did untold damage to both myself and the Name of Jesus. Again the Lord called me, and from that moment I have followed, and according to the light he gave me, I consecrated myself at that time to him. But I found that I was not living the overcoming life. With the baptism in the Spirit, God came in, not merely as 'Resident" but as President. Then I discovered the Apostolic message, I was now in the valley of dry bones. God led me and convinced me in my own kitchen of his own church order. The beauty of the home is order, and I sought the scriptures to see if these things were so. There was no doubt about it, I was still willing to follow him and found myself, and him, in the "pre-historic church".[90]

(Mrs J. McKeown)

Jot down anything you feel God might be saying to you personally.

_____

_____

_____

_____

_____

_____

Thank you, Lord for leading me, and changing my life.

---

[90] 1939.

Day 77: Spiritual Authority

Further reading
Eph. 6

One day the evil spirit answered them, "Jesus I know, and Paul I know about, but who are you?" Acts 19:15 (NIV)

And whatever you ask in prayer, you will receive, if you have faith. Matt 21:22 (ESV)

Demons should be dealt with in the power of the Holy Spirit and not in the natural man. Thank God! There is deliverance from all the power of the devil or demons. Jesus on the cross spoiled principalities and powers for us, and his victory is to be our victory, for he displayed his power as a victory for us. Thank God! This power is still operative in the church of God to those who will believe. Wherever there is true faith, God will meet the need. Many in the church today can testify of awesome deliverances from demonic powers and all the work of the enemy. To God be all the praise and glory![91]

(Frank Hodges)

Jot down anything you feel God might be saying to you personally.

_____

_____

_____

_____

_____

_____

Thank you, Father that in Jesus there is victory and authority over all the power of the enemy. The cross has disarmed the rulers and principalities of the present dark world.

---

[91] Apostle Frank Hodges 1932.

Day 78: Character Building

Further reading
Romans 5

**Endurance produces character, and character produces hope.
Romans 5:4 (ESV)**

The ultimate purpose of every ministry is to build character. If we have no character, we have nothing that is worth talking about. Character is not mere morality. We can be moral without character. Character is nothing else than the impartation of the divine life and the divine nature, and participation in the communicable attributes of God. We are responsible for building character; no one can build it for us. No man has ever gained success or become "self-made" without a lot of toil, labour and self-denial. Think of Sir Henry Jones: the son of the Blacksmith in North Wales. He found himself in the chair of philosophy in the University of Glasgow. But between the blacksmith's shop and the university, Sir Henry knew something of toil, labour and self-denial. It is just the same in character building. We will never have a God-pleasing character without toil, suffering, agony, pain, groaning and self-denial.[92]

(T. Rees)

Jot down anything you feel God might be saying to you personally.

_____

_____

_____

_____

_____

_____

Father, help me to work with you, and not against you, in seasons of suffering so that Christ may be formed within me.

---

[92] Apostle T Rees 1932

Day 79: The Cross

Further reading
Isaiah 53

For our sake he made him to be sin who knew no sin, so that in him we might become the righteousness of God. 2 Corinthians 5:21 (ESV)

Don't leave the cross! Don't leave the place where the greatest expression of my heart was revealed to you. It is at the cross alone I can meet with you in the deepest spiritual sense. It is not in the joy and the enthusiasm, so much, although that is well and good – I have come to give you joy as a portion of your inheritance – but it is at the cross where I can melt your heart. It is at the cross where I can break your spirit. It is at the cross where I can bend your will. It is at the cross where I can mould your motives. It is at the cross where I can create those desires that can spring up into righteousness and a holy life. Come to the cross, I will meet you face to face.[93]

(J.D Eynon)

Jot down anything you feel God might be saying to you personally.

_____

_____

_____

_____

_____

_____

Jesus, keep me near the cross, there a precious fountain, free to all—a healing stream, flows from Calv'ry's mountain.

In the cross, in the cross, be my glory ever; from the cross my ransomed soul, nothing then shall sever.[94]

---

[93] Prophet, J.D Eynon 1938.

[94] Hymn.

Day 80: What Jesus means to me

Now may the God of peace who brought again from the dead our Lord Jesus, the great shepherd of the sheep, by the blood of the eternal covenant, equip you with everything good that you may do his will, working in us that which is pleasing in his sight, through Jesus Christ, to whom be glory forever and ever. Amen. Hebrews 13:20-21 (ESV)

I want to speak of Jesus and what he means to me and what he should mean to you also. It was love that brought Jesus to die for us on the cross. It was love that brought him down from the Glory. Another thing we see in Jesus' sacrifice is humility. He made himself of no reputation, that he might lift the beggar from the gutter, and make the king on his throne a humble worshipper and follower. The next thing we have is a wonderful security in our Lord Jesus Christ. Security spells **shelter** to us. When the waves of tribulation come against us, there is a sure shelter in the cleft of the rock.[95]

(I. Martin)

Jot down anything you feel God might be saying to you personally.

_____

_____

_____

_____

_____

_____

_____

You hide my soul in the cleft of the rock, that shadows a dry, thirsty land; You hide my life in the depths of Your love, And cover me there with your hand, And cover me there with your hand.[96]

---

[95] Bro. I. Martin, Paisley.

[96] Hymn.

Day 81: Praying in the Holy Spirit

Further reading
Eph. 1:15-23

Your kingdom come, your will be done, on earth as it is in heaven. Matthew 6:10 (ESV)

But you, beloved, building yourselves up on your most holy faith, praying in the Holy Spirit. Jude 1:20 (NASB)

Praying in the Holy Spirit is spiritual prayer, a thing of the soul, and the whole attitude of life. This idea of praying is so different from the attitude of the Pharisee, who loved long prayers, especially in public. There is a similar thought behind pagan prayers – time, place and ritual being the main factors. How different is the exhortation: praying in the Holy Spirit. The reward of our prayer is power to pray. A prayerful spirit is a life in secret communion with the Father. Prayer is not a part time job to be done by fits and starts. Prayer is a thing of the whole life, a heart of worship. Prayer brings God into our life.[97]

(A. Gardiner)

Jot down anything you feel God might be saying to you personally.

_____

_____

_____

_____

_____

_____

Lord, teach me what it is to pray in the Spirit. Lead me into deep intercession. Help me partner with you by my prayers. Lead me to pray for the things that you want to see accomplished.

---

[97] Apostle, A. Gardiner, 1931.

Day 82: Tabernacle

Further reading
Romans 12

Do not be conformed to this world, but be transformed by the renewal of your mind, that by testing you may discern what is the will of God, what is good and acceptable and perfect. Romans 12:2 (ESV)

Everything in nature lives on its environment. The little flower lives on the elements in the air. The Christian can only spiritually live as he inhales and takes into himself the very essence and nature and attributes and principles of God. Thank God, that we, his people, have been brought to life by his Spirit, and we've been restored to fellowship with him. But that is only the beginning. He wants to impart into every heart principles of truth, righteousness, light, life and victory. All this is in him. And when he becomes the environment of our souls, we participate in the life of the Spirit. He strengthens us by his Spirit in the inner man, so that Christ may make his abode or tabernacle with us.[98]

(D.P. Williams)

Jot down anything you feel God might be saying to you personally.

_____

_____

_____

_____

_____

_____

Thank you Lord that you have delivered me from the kingdom of darkness, and translated me into the kingdom of your Son. Thank you that your Spirit dwells in me.

---

[98] Apostle, D.P. Williams, 1932.

Day 83: Holy Glory

Further reading
1 Chron. 16

**Seek the Lord and his strength; seek his presence continually!
1 Chronicles 16:11 (ESV)**

I appeal to you therefore, brothers, by the mercies of God, to present your bodies as a living sacrifice, holy and acceptable to God, which is your spiritual worship. Romans 12:1 (ESV)

I have come to reveal my holiness. Because I am causing you to see my Glory, and causing the revelation of holiness to come within your reach, there is a possibility that you will become discouraged because I am revealing myself. But I declare to you that there is no need for any soul to leave my presence without that energy you came to seek. As it is written, "Seek and you shall find." I have come to meet the need, to send you away rejoicing in the fullness of my Glory.[99]

(J.McCabe)

Jot down anything you feel God might be saying to you personally.

_____

_____

_____

_____

_____

_____

Triune God, help me to draw near to you. Cleanse me with the blood of Jesus, draw me near to the throne, and fill me to overflowing, in Jesus' Name I pray.

---

[99] J.McAbe, Scotland 1932.

Day 84: Have you received? (Part 1)

Further reading
Acts 19

He said unto them, Have ye received the Holy Ghost since ye believed? And they said unto him, We have not so much as heard whether there be any Holy Ghost. Acts 19:2 (KJV)

As the majority of my readers are by no means strangers to the *apostolic vision*, although some may lack the fullness of a pentecostal experience, it is not my intent to spend a long preamble on what we mean when we speak of the baptism of the Holy Spirit. It is surely quite sufficient to affirm uncompromisingly that we believe in an experience which is not one bit less miraculous or spectacular than that which the converts of the early apostolic days enjoyed. We believe, that today, as then, the incoming of the Holy Spirit into a person's life, is attended by miraculous signs affecting the whole of his or her life and behaviour, not least of which, is the initial scriptural evidence of 'speaking in tongues.'[100]

(E.H Williams)

Jot down anything you feel God might be saying to you personally.

_____

_____

_____

_____

_____

_____

Father, fill me afresh with your Spirit, and release your gifts in me and through me. Let there be nothing lacking in my life. Help me walk in all that Jesus died to give me.

---

[100] Pastor, E.H Williams, 1962.

Day 85: Have you received? (Part 2)

Further reading
Acts 11

As I began to speak, the Holy Spirit came on them as he had come on us at the beginning. Acts 11:15 (NIV)

When Paul placed his hands on them, the Holy Spirit came on them, and they spoke in tongues and prophesied. Acts 19:6 (NIV)

The challenge of our text (Acts 19:2), coming as it did, some 20 years after Pentecost, is very thought provoking indeed. A pentecostal experience is available – I would suggest imperatively essential, but here we find a small group of struggling Christians who are in need and confess: "We have not so much as heard whether there be any Holy Spirit." What a tragedy! But how much more of a tragedy to realise that some of us, with pentecostal backgrounds over the years, with a theoretical concept of the value of such an experience, are just carrying on the daily round of Christian living devoid of any real thirst for this divinely ordained Spirit Baptism?[101]

(E.H Williams)

Jot down anything you feel God might be saying to you personally.

_____

_____

_____

_____

_____

_____

Come Holy Spirit!

---

[101] Ibid.

Day 86: Have you received? (Part 3)

Further reading
Galatians 5

After they prayed, the place where they were meeting was shaken. And they were all filled with the Holy Spirit and spoke the word of God boldly. Acts 4:31 (NIV)

Nevertheless I tell you the truth. It is to your advantage that I go away; for if I do not go away, the Helper will not come to you; but if I depart, I will send Him to you. John 16:7 (NKJV)

These are the words of the Son of God; implying, or rather, asserting, that the coming Spirit was preferable to his own physical presence among them as disciples. To put it simply, it was imperative that the God who was WITH them, (The Son of God) should depart to enable God to be IN them, in the person of God the Holy Spirit. Have *you* received the Holy Spirit? Has God come to INDWELL you?

(E.H Williams)

Jot down anything you feel God might be saying to you personally.

_____

_____

_____

_____

_____

_____

Holy Spirit, help me to get to know you. Forgive me for the times I have grieved you or quenched you. Teach me to be sensitive to you.

Day 87: Have you received? (Part 4)

Further reading
1 Cor. 3

Don't you know that you yourselves are God's temple and that God's Spirit dwells in your midst? 1 Corinthians 3:16 (NIV)

If you then, though you are evil, know how to give good gifts to your children, how much more will your Father in heaven give the Holy Spirit to those who ask him! Luke 11:13 (NIV)

The first essential condition for receiving the Baptism in the Holy Spirit is ABSOLUTE SURRENDER to the Lord. I do not mean at this stage, surrender to the will of God for your life, although that is of course vital in Christian experience. What we need is consciously to completely surrender ourselves, body, soul and spirit, to the Lord as we tarry before him for his fullness. How often do we see the Spirit coming upon a person causing him or her to start to shake and quake? It seems that God the Holy Spirit is fighting his way in to take possession of the citadel of that person's being, whilst the fear of man, the fear of loss of reputation, the fear of making a mistake, prevents absolute surrender to the Incoming One.

(E.H Williams)

Jot down anything you feel God might be saying to you personally.

_____

_____

_____

_____

_____

_____

Father in heaven, I bow before you and lift up my hands in absolute surrender – take my life and let it be, wholly consecrated to thee. May your Spirit take possession of every part of me.

Day 88: Have you received? (Part 5)

Further reading
James 1

But let him ask In faith, with no doubting, for he who doubts is like a wave of the sea driven and tossed by the wind. For let not that man suppose that he will receive anything from the Lord; he is a double-minded man, unstable in all his ways.
James 1:6-8) (NKJV)

It was the Apostle James who warns us of the importance of the prayer of faith. Without faith, it is not only impossible to please God, but also impossible to receive anything from him. Faith goes much deeper than belief.

The need is not merely a faith in the existence of a Spirit baptism. Not just a faith in the necessity of such a baptism. Not only faith that the Lord has not changed his methods, and still baptises today. The great need is FAITH that the Lord WILL fulfil to us personally, as individuals, his own promise. This faith will spring from the Word of God. Active faith will blossom into actual acceptance. God gives; we must receive, before we can become possessors.[102]

(E.H Williams)

Jot down anything you feel God might be saying to you personally.

_____

_____

_____

_____

_____

_____

Thank you Lord that you are more willing to give, than I am to receive. Help me walk in faith.

---

[102] Ibid.

Day 89: The Five-fold Ministry (Part 1) Further reading
Eph. 4:1-13

He who descended is the very one who ascended higher than all the heavens, in order to fill the whole universe. Eph 4:10 (NIV)

God's governmental jurisdiction flows from the Head (Christ) to the Body (the church) through the various vital functions known as ministry gifts which are not only ministerial and supernatural, but governmental in their operation. Through all these ministries, the will of God is revealed. For example, through the lips of the evangelist, is made known, by the gospel of grace, God's will to save. Through the pastor the will of God is revealed, showing God's shepherd care for his sheep, for his will is to foster and feed the flock of God. Through the teacher, the will of God is shown in the scriptures, both precept and practice. Then the prophet, together with the apostle, is a vital governmental function for the expression of the will of the Head. For both receive revelation by the Spirit respecting the purpose and plan of God, as it relates to the Body, and often to persons and places.[103]

(C.C. Ireson)

Jot down anything you feel God might be saying to you personally.

_____

_____

_____

_____

_____

_____

Father, thank you that Jesus is the one who rules over his church. Thank you that the church is led by Jesus and he will preserve his church and bring it to maturity and fullness.

---

[103] Pastor, C.C. Ireson, 1958.

Day 90: The Five-fold Ministry (Part 2)

Further reading
Eph. 4:9-16

So Christ himself gave the apostles, the prophets, the evangelists, the pastors and teachers, to equip his people for works of service, so that the body of Christ may be built up (Ephesians 4:11-12 (NIV)

Whilst the Headship of Christ expresses itself through all the valued five-fold ministries, the apostleship is something indispensable to the Body's perfecting, without which the Body is impaired and incomplete. I have observed after 45 years' experience of the Baptism of the Spirit, that pentecostal churches, whilst holding to the baptism of the Holy Spirit, and to many other vital truths, lack apostleship and the prophetic office. I heard a prominent leader of one of the groups say about three years ago, "We lack leadership! We seem to be afraid of the word; I don't know why we should be afraid of it." I thought to myself that he was unconsciously expressing the lack of Apostleship, though of course he never used the word. Perhaps he was afraid of it. Of course, leadership is not necessarily Apostleship, yet Apostleship has leadership and true leadership is that which mostly contributes to the welfare of the led. True leadership is strong, sincere, courageous, careful, clear, bold after decision, unshaken by rumour of failure, far-sighted, and not seeking personal gain.[104]

(C.C. Ireson)

Jot down anything you feel God might be saying to you personally.

_____

_____

_____

_____

_____

_____

Thank you for leaders, strengthen my local church leaders today.

---

[104] Ibid.

Day 91: Old-Time Fire

Further reading
Hebrews 4

For the word of God is living and active, sharper than any two-edged sword, piercing to the division of soul and of spirit, of joints and of marrow, and discerning the thoughts and intentions of the heart. Hebrews 4:12 (ESV)

When he comes, he will prove the world to be in the wrong about sin and righteousness and judgment. John 16:8 (NIV)

Today the church is trying to convince the world of its origin, existence and commission by its multiple constitutions and various polities. Judging the church today by the early church, it seems that it has gone back to live in that period between Easter and Pentecost – and behind closed doors is fighting hard for its existence. Things are so different when the Holy Spirit comes! "Oh Holy Ghost, Revival comes from thee!" When the Holy Spirit came, he took full control. The early church never tried to control the mighty power and manifestation of the Spirit of God. It seems that they knew they could not![105]

(Thomas Rees)

Jot down anything you feel God might be saying to you personally.

_____

_____

_____

_____

_____

_____

Let the fire fall, let the fire fall, let the fire from heaven fall,
We are waiting and expecting, now in faith, dear Lord we call;
Let the fire fall, let the fire fall, on thy promise we depend;
From the glory of thy presence, let the Pentecostal fire descend.[106]

---

[105] Pastor, Thomas Rees, 1939.

[106] Hymn.

Day 92: The Power of Jesus

Further reading
John 6

For this is the will of my Father, that everyone who looks on the Son and believes In him should have eternal life, and I will raise him up on the last day. John 6:40 (ESV)

Jesus is just the same today. If you can understand the love of Jesus – one day he is honoured, praised, and adored; the next day he is despised, forsaken and rejected by people. Although Jesus had attracted the multitudes to himself, by his wonderful miracles, and by his wonderful preaching, the tables are soon turned and many of those who sung his praise now follow him no longer. What caused John (the vindictive son of thunder) who wanted to call fire down from heaven to destroy the Samaritans, to declare: "See what manner of love God has bestowed on us that we should be called sons of God." It was the mighty power of God. What is it that delivered the blaspheming Peter, who cursed and swore before a little servant girl, but who afterwards delivered that sermon on the day of Pentecost when 3000 got saved? It was the mighty power of God. That same power can deliver your soul, no matter how deeply stained your sins are because the blood of Christ, God's Son, can cleanse every one of them.[107]

(D.S. Armstrong)

Jot down anything you feel God might be saying to you personally.

_____

_____

_____

_____

_____

_____

Lord today I want to bring before you people that I know who need to experience your life changing power. I bring _____ *before you. Meet with them, Jesus!*

---

[107] Pastor, D.S. Armstrong,

Day 93: Redemption

Further reading
Romans 6

"For God so loved the world, that he gave his only Son, that whoever believes in him should not perish but have eternal life. John 3:16 (ESV)

At the cross we see sin at its worst. The heavenly Lamb was murdered, not by savages who knew no better, but by the most religious men of the most religious nation, outside the most religious city in the world. It was done illegally, it was done callously, it was done in the very name of religion. The pure, loving, compassionate, healing Lord was savagely and heartlessly done to death. Yet at the cross we see love at its best. The eternal Word is dumb; omnipotence yields itself up, there is complete submission. While the fires of eternal justice are burning themselves out on the infinite sacrifice, the eternal heart is radiating forgiveness. Through the fruit of a tree, man fell; on a barren tree, nailed, wounded, and dying, the great redeeming rose of divine love blossomed out, and humanity was lifted back to God.[108]

(W.A.C. Rowe)

Jot down anything you feel God might be saying to you personally.

_____

_____

_____

_____

_____

_____

When I survey the wondrous cross, On which the Prince of Glory died, My richest gain I count but loss, And pour contempt on all my pride.[109]

---

[108] Pastor, W.A.C. Rowe, 1939.

[109] Hymn.

Day 94: Apostolic Worship (Part 1)

Further reading
1 Cor. 14:1-5

What then shall we say, brothers and sisters? When you come together, each of you has a hymn, or a word of instruction, a revelation, a tongue or an interpretation. Everything must be done so that the church may be built up. 1 Corinthians 14:26 (NIV)

In this passage we have a glimpse of the apostolic form of Christian worship. The New Testament writers knew nothing at all of an individualistic Christianity. It is true that the salvation of the soul must, of necessity, be an individual experience. But the believer, who has been saved through faith in Christ, seeks the fellowship of his brothers and sisters. No one can grow towards spiritual maturity in isolation. This is why the Apostles of the Lord Jesus insisted upon the assembling together of the Saints: "And let us consider how we may spur one another on toward love and good deeds, not giving up meeting together, as some are in the habit of doing, but encouraging one another—and all the more as you see the Day approaching." Heb. 10:24-25[110]

(D. Kongo)

Jot down anything you feel God might be saying to you personally.

_____

_____

_____

_____

_____

_____

Lord thank you for your people, thank you for your house, thank you for the church!

---

[110] Pastor D. Kongo, 1926.

Day 95: Apostolic Worship (Part 2)

Further reading
1 Cor.14: 6-12

Beloved friends, what does all this imply? When you conduct your meetings, you should always let everything be done to build up the church family. Whether you share a song of praise, a teaching, a divine revelation, or a tongue and interpretation, let each one contribute what strengthens others.
1 Corinthians 14:26 (TPT)

These people had gathered together to worship God. Their place of worship was not a grand cathedral, nor even a strongly built chapel. It was an ordinary room, of an ordinary house, of one of the ordinary brethren, and everything in it extraordinarily ordinary. Neither was there a raised platform, nor an altar of any kind, and above all, there was not even the least shadow of the modern pulpit. Every member was on the same floor, worshipping the same God, and serving the same king. Having gathered together, we presume, in good time, with grateful hearts, and on fire for God, the leader opens the meeting through prayer, calling on God to manifest His presence among His people.[111]

(D. Kongo)

Jot down anything you feel God might be saying to you personally.

_____

_____

_____

_____

_____

_____

Thank you God that we all have a part to play. Help me to use my gifts to serve your saints.

---

[111] Ibid.

Day 96: Apostolic Worship (Part 3)

Further reading
1 Cor. 14:13-19

I thank God that I speak In tongues more than all of you. 19 But in the church I would rather speak five intelligible words to instruct others than ten thousand words in a tongue. 1 Corinthians 14:18 (NIV)

All the members present are spiritually alive, and submissive, to the promptings of the Holy Spirit; and everyone moved to action, through the divine inspiration of God. At the close of the service, every member with a heart overflowing with joy, and faces shining with the light not of this world, would return home refreshed, inspired and encouraged on their pilgrimage towards the land of pure delight. Further, one of the things in this worship is variety: "Each has…a psalm, a tongue, an interpretation, a revelation…" There is nothing monotonous about this service, but every member contributing their share, as led by the Holy Spirit.[112]

(D. Kongo)

Jot down anything you feel God might be saying to you personally.

_____

_____

_____

_____

_____

_____

Thank you Lord for all the gifts of the Spirit, thank you also that these gifts are not for personal benefit, but for the good of your people.

---

[112] Ibid.

Day 97: Apostolic Worship (Part 4)

Further reading
1 Cor. 14:20-25

Whenever you come together, each of you has a psalm... 1 Corinthians 14:26 (NKJV)

Sing to the LORD a new song; sing to the LORD, all the earth. Psalm 96:1 (NIV)

This is not of necessity an Old Testament Psalm, although we presume that Old Testament Psalms were used too, as the saints were prompted by the Spirit. The psalm Paul has in mind, we believe, is the psalm that resembled the Old Testament ones in their production – the product of the Spirit for the occasion, something like the Song of Mary: "My soul does magnify the Lord." This is the expression of the heart filled with and illuminated by the Holy Spirit of God. [113]

(D. Kongo)

Jot down anything you feel God might be saying to you personally.

_____

_____

_____

_____

_____

_____

Thank you Jesus for the power of singing your praise. Fill my heart with the songs of Zion. May my heart be overflowing with the songs of salvation. Let praise pour forth from my lips like a river!

---

[113] Ibid.

Day 98: Apostolic Worship (Part 5)

Further reading
1 Cor. 14:26-28

Whenever you come together, each of you… has a teaching…a revelation…1 Corinthians 14:26 (NKJV)

Let the message of Christ dwell among you richly as you teach and admonish one another with all wisdom through psalms, hymns, and songs from the Spirit, singing to God with gratitude in your hearts. Colossians 3:16

Worship is not all singing. Teaching also follows the Psalm, and it is only the joyful heart that is open to receiving the doctrine. In the book of Acts we read that the church devoted themselves to "the Apostles doctrine." This teaching would be in harmony with that.

We also read that one has a "revelation". It seems clear that Paul links this revelation with prophecy: "But if anything is revealed to another who sits by, let the first keep silent." The Holy Spirit of God takes hold of the mind, as well as the language of the individual, to speak forth the hidden secrets of God to his people.[114]

(D. Kongo)

Jot down anything you feel God might be saying to you personally.

_____

_____

_____

_____

_____

_____

Praise you Father for the word of truth. Your word brings life and light into my life. Your word brings order and stability. Your word brings revelation and transformation.

---

[114] Ibid.

Day 99: Apostolic Worship (Part 6)

Further reading
1 Cor. 14:29-33

Whenever you come together, each of you... has a tongue...has an interpretation...1 Corinthians 14:26 (NKJV)

Therefore let him who speaks in a tongue pray that he may interpret. 1 Corinthians 14:13

Tongues are an ecstatic utterance entirely beyond the reason of man, and therefore the highest form of ecstasy. Sometimes the whole congregation would sing praises in this new tongue, everyone thereby receiving a personal blessing of soul. And there is also the gift of interpretation which is given to interpret the new tongue for strengthening and comforting the church. What a variety in one meeting! All are in perfect harmony, led by One Spirit. Where has this variety gone today? The Spirit has not withdrawn his presence! Neither have the gifts granted to the primitive church been done away with, except in the professing Christian church where the wisdom of man holds sway. Never-the-less, in spite of the irreverent handling of 'Worldly Wiseman', we are convinced that the Apostolic form of Christian worship is the only true one for every age. It is so simple, so spiritual, so divine, plenty of variety, yet perfect unity, leading to oneness of mind, humility of spirit, and purity of heart. [115]

(D. Kongo)

Jot down anything you feel God might be saying to you personally.

_____

_____

_____

_____

_____

_____

Thank you Father for the gift of tongues, please release the fullness of this gift in my life, in Jesus' Name.

---

[115] Ibid.

Day 100: The Burning Bush

Further reading
Acts 7:30-34

After forty years had passed, an angel appeared to Moses In the flames of a burning bush in the desert near Mount Sinai. 31 When he saw this, he was amazed at the sight. As he went over to get a closer look, he heard the Lord... Acts 7:30 (NIV)

Why are my people so inconsistent? Why do they play, like children, in the midst of the burning bush? They remain selfishly with themselves, refusing to see and hear the voice from the burning bush proclaiming: Go! I am moving a specially chosen people to reach the multitudes in my way, according to my word. As the doors open, you must go through! Do not play with the holy things (gifts, positions, offices) I will not be hindered for much longer by childishness. The demands are too important. The congregation of the people of God is aflame with the fire of love towards me and my will. I declare that I have a people in whom I delight, and as long as I delight in my people: Behold! I am going to work through them, and I will accomplish the infinite contents of my promises.[116]

(W. Jones Williams)

Jot down anything you feel God might be saying to you personally.

_____

_____

_____

_____

_____

_____

Lord, thank you for these extracts from the apostolic movement – raise up a fresh apostolic work in our day. We pray for a resurgence of full-blown New Testament Christianity – in Jesus' Name!

---

[116] Prophet, W. Jones Williams, 1932.

The following eleven statements were developed by early Apostolic Church leaders and remain as key points of belief, expressing in simple and systematic terms, what the Apostolic Church holds to as sound Biblical truth.

1. The one true and living God who eternally exists in three persons in unity: Father, Son and Holy Spirit.

2. The inherent corruptness of man through the Fall; The necessity of repentance and regeneration by grace and through faith in Christ alone and the eternal separation from God of the finally unrepentant.

3. The Virgin birth, sinless life, atoning death, triumphant resurrection, ascension and continuing intercession of our Lord Jesus Christ; His second coming and millennial reign upon earth.

4. The Justification and sanctification of believers through the finished work of Christ.

5. The baptism of the Holy spirit for believers with supernatural signs, empowering the church for its mission in the world.

6. The gifts of the Holy Spirit for the building up of the Church and ministry to the world.

7. The Sacraments of Baptism by immersion and of the Lord's Supper

8. The divine inspiration and authority of the Holy Scriptures.

9. Christ's leadership of the Church through apostles, prophets, evangelists, pastors, teachers, elders and deacons, for unity, maturity and growth of the church.

10. The security of the believer as he remains in Christ

11. The privilege and responsibility of bringing tithes and offerings to the Lord.[117]

---

[117] http://apostolic-church.org/about-us/tenets/

Thank you for purchasing a copy of this book.

50% of the royalties will be donated to Connect 2 Forth Valley. A new Teen Challenge Ministry that is being developed in the Forth Valley area.

If you enjoyed this book, you can help us raise more money for Teen Challenge by telling friends and family members about the book, sharing a link to the book on social media and writing a review on Amazon.

If you are interested in buying a number of copies of 'Vision from the Valleys' you can contact John in the flowing ways:

Email: jcaldwellskye@gmail.com

Facebook: @JohnCaldwell80

Instagram: jonboycaldwell

Twitter: @jonjcaldwell

Other books by John Caldwell

Many communities are ravaged by problems associated with poverty, crime and drug and alcohol abuse. Substantial answers to the urban crisis are all but non-existent. 'Christ, the Cross and the Concrete Jungle' is the story of a young man's deliverance from a lifestyle of desperation and delinquency to a new life of freedom and hope. This book reveals the remarkable journey of transformation and redemption that is made possible through the gospel of Jesus Christ.

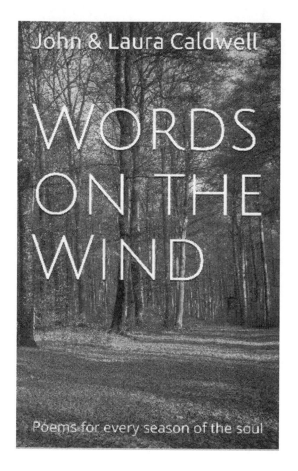

John & Laura Caldwell

WORDS ON THE WIND

Poems for every season of the soul

Written at various times and stages, these poems reflect the different seasons of the Christian life. Each poem reflects not only the shifting seasons, but the unchanging God whose love never changes. Whatever season you are in, these poems will encourage you to keep trusting God because his purposes for you are good.

Printed in Poland
by Amazon Fulfillment
Poland Sp. z o.o., Wrocław

49506635R00072